ON YOUR OWN TERMS

Building a Sustainable, Value-Creating Business

PRAISE FOR
ON YOUR OWN TERMS

"The MORE process has provided our leadership team with a clear direction and defined model to follow with clear steps and measurements. This book is a MUST-read for small business owners needing a push to maximize business value and turn their dream for a succession plan into a reality."

Jeff Murphy
President and CEO, ECT Services, Inc.

"This book is a must-read for any business owner experiencing the challenges of continual growth. It teaches you the benefit of reevaluating your management style and getting advice from leadership experts."

Daron Stockton
Chick-fil-A Operator

ON YOUR OWN TERMS

Building a Sustainable, Value-Creating Business

Getting
MORE™
from Your
Business

**Lee Quinn
and Lewis Rudy**

DEDICATION

From Lee Quinn

To John and Mary Lou Quinn, my parents, who encouraged me to make my own decisions and showed me the value of the important things in life. And to Wendy, the love of my life, who has been by my side through thick and thin.

From Lewis Rudy

To my parents, who trusted me and let me take chances to figure out the impossible. To my hard-working, broad-thinking, loving sons. And to my love Amy, for all her support and encouragement.

ACKNOWLEDGMENTS

From Lee Quinn

I want to pay tribute to the team at my family's business. This story would never have happened without your trust, loyalty, and hard work. Special thanks to Cathy Fyock, My Biz Book Strategist and Possibility Partner; without you, I would not have made this journey. My thanks to Amy Romines, who kept us on track, developed the Rudy curve and was a great editor-in-chief. Without exception, our editors were fantastic; thanks to Mark Ray, Brent Densford, Jeff Murphy, Daron Stockton, and Hilary Jastram, and also to our book designer, Courtney Hudson. And finally, and certainly not last in my mind, is Kate Colbert at Silver Tree Publishing — you have provided us with invaluable advice, guidance, and helped us finish strong.

From Lewis Rudy

I have worked with so many business owners and people who were trying to figure it out! I am thankful for their trust in us to make what could be considered the greatest change in their thinking, leadership, and methods. I truly applaud their courage and am grateful for every time they dug deep to take the chance on change. And a special thanks to Lee Quinn for his leadership in the endeavor of this book. I am proud to call you partner.

TABLE OF CONTENTS

LETTER TO THE READER: MY STORY

I was probably like you. I thought my family manufacturing business was unique. We were a consumer durable goods manufacturer that sold through retailers to consumers. Our business had so many nuances that it would be impossible for an outsider to ever understand how it ran. There was an art to running the business, and no one could do it like we could. We were successful, and we challenged ourselves enough to grow moderately and maintain modest profitability. It was a comfortable and agreeable way to make a living.

But in my mind, I faced uncomfortable questions: *Where was this business going? What did I really think was going to happen to it?* I was constantly anxious, frustrated, uncomfortable, and uncertain about the direction of our business. In fact, the only time I didn't worry was when I was fighting fires at work. That was a great diversion from the real questions, letting me focus on the eight to 10 people waiting on me when I arrived at the factory. But when the fires were out, the doubts returned. We were getting product shipped and making sales. Why was that not enough?

I was the CEO of the business, and I was responsible for growing it and providing acceptable profits. I was responsible for the business and the 70-plus families who were dependent on it for their living.

But we were stuck in the mud. We had always done things the same way. "Great idea, but it won't work" was our mantra, and "When did you hear that? Why was I not told that?" was a constant refrain. Information was protected and disseminated on a need-to-know basis — and no one needed to know. The business was not being managed to be a sustainable, growth-oriented, value-creating entity. But shouldn't that be the purpose of a family business? If it is, then we needed to change the way we thought about and worked in our business.

Goals? We thought we didn't need any goals other than to increase sales and profit. What about reducing operating costs, material decreases, sales increases, profit increases? How were we going to accomplish those? Plan? We didn't need no stinking plan. If we *did* have a plan, it was executed but not sustained. A good plan lasted 30, 60, 90 days and then died. And it didn't even get the recognition of a Viking funeral. Instead, it passed gently into the night, never to be seen again.

The pace of our business was accelerating at an astronomical rate that was increasing every day. Our customers were either dying on the vine, being absorbed into larger entities, or being sold through other marketing channels. Entire new marketing channels were taking market share. The piece of the pie we could compete for was becoming smaller every day. The time-to-market and change-to-market time were frighteningly fast. We would begin a new product-line-introduction cycle before the last one was even completed. It was driving me crazy. We were always reacting to our environment instead of strategically planning and executing.

What's more, our family was the largest lender to the business. How were we going to pay ourselves off — given the demands of capital for sales growth and capital expenditures — to keep up with the market? Where was that cash going to come from? We were already "all-in" from a family financial aspect.

And we, the owners, were not getting any younger. Where was the next generation of leaders? Who was going to replace us as CEO, president of sales and marketing manager, and CFO? How long were we going to have to work to have what we wanted from the business? How were my family and I going to get paid out past my transition from the company?

There is one truth we cannot escape: we will all exit our businesses one way or the other. Was I going to exit on my terms or just accept whatever happened along the way?

Does this sound like your business? Do you question the direction, trajectory, and velocity of your business? How can real change to your business add material value?

This book tells the story of our family's successful business and the process that changed its trajectory and movement. The journey brought us to a place where we had options for the business and ourselves. It enabled us to capitalize on them and ultimately allowed us to exit the business on our own terms and pursue other dreams.

This book could also be the story of *your* business and how it grew to be successful. The secret is not just in asking the hard questions but in answering them. And the secret is in following the Master of Reverse Engineering (MORE™) process.

Reverse engineering is the process of taking something apart, examining and documenting the parts and information that you extracted, and putting it back together. MORE™ has one additional facet: it puts the business back together in a new way to meet its goals. It changes the business and its direction. MORE™ is transformational.

Real change is what MORE™ is all about. It's a holistic process to equip your business for sustainable success. It draws information from your business, addresses change in real time, and produces a business equipped to meet your goals and expectations. It allows you to manage your business to be a sustainable, value-creating entity.

MORE™ forced us to look at our entire business as a complete entity with multiple functions and processes. We first defined success for us, the owners, and for the business. We then took the business apart down to its functions and processes and determined if, in their current form, they strategically met our defined goals or could produce results that took us to our goals. Every aspect and process in our business was examined. We set our sights and focused on the actions that were most urgent while prioritizing the others. All our actions and plans happened within the context of the success goals we had set.

MORE™ looks at every aspect of the business in respect to your vision and goals. It questions and challenges your current thinking about structure, processes, and direction. Is the business meeting your expectations? How does it need to change to meet those expectations?

MORE™ begins when you, the owner, ask yourself what your vision of success for the business is. Is it meeting your current expectations? What do you want it to look like next year, in three years, and in five years? How do you want the business to operate daily to create growth, profit, and success? What will be the result of all the hard work in the end? What is the end goal? You will exit your business one way or another. How do you want to exit the business?

The MORE™ journey requires courage, focus, and perseverance. It's a painful journey of introspection about the operation of your business. You may realize, as I did, that you are the one holding back your creation from being all that it can be. Changing yourself, your thinking about the business, and the business itself is an arduous process. It takes a team and teamwork. It is a no-holds-barred journey. But it can lead to a sustainable, value-creating business — and many fewer uncomfortable questions about the future.

— *Lee Quinn*

P.S. You'll notice as you're reading this book that it's told from a first-person point of view, from my perspective unless otherwise noted. But the MORE™ process is the brain child of my colleague and mentor Lewis Rudy and this book, therefore, would not have been possible without him.

CHAPTER 1
The Beginning is the End

The Place to Start

Let's start at the very beginning, "a very good place to start." (So goes the song from *The Sound of Music*.) But in our case, it's the wrong place to start. Everyone wants to know "Who did it?" in a mystery. What happened? This is the end of our story.

The End: December 2016

The "signing" of the documents and the close of the sale was something of an anticlimax. I'd had a vision of everyone — the purchasers, lawyers, and accountants — sitting around a table as documents were signed, checks would be passed between the parties, and handshakes shared all around.

Not! The documents were signed on Saturday the week before closing. The lawyers were on the phone with each other the day of and the day after closing, dotting the i's and crossing the t's. We owners were sitting in our offices as the money was transmitted in bits and bytes over the Internet to various bank accounts, just minutes before those systems were shut down. The commands for transfer were given over a cell phone to bank officers sitting at their computers.

That was not quite the glamorous ending I had envisioned for the day I would walk away from the business after 38 years, no longer an owner. However, our family business of 59 years had been success-fully sold to a strategic buyer, creating a wealth of opportunities for the family and its owners. All the hard work we'd put into making our business a sustainable entity had paid off. It felt good — even if it hadn't happened as I'd imagined.

History of My Family Business

Our family business was started in 1958 by my grandfather, father, and uncle. They had been part of another similar manufacturing business, one my grandfather had the foresight to see was not going in the right direction.

Our family business was conceived on the back porch of the family home on a hot August night. My grandfather told my father and my uncle, "I don't think this business has a future for you. We are going to start one of our own." He was referring to a business that he had been a partner in since the 1920s. With that statement and my grand-mother's inheritance, my grandfather, at 65 years of age, launched a business that would remain in our family for 59 more years.

Our family leadership team at the time of the final transaction of exiting the business, was the third generation: me (the oldest) and my two brothers. At the time of the sale, I had worked in the business for 38 years. My next brother in birth order joined the business after his college career, during which he worked part-time at a furniture retailer. Our youngest brother had had a successful career as a lawyer, practicing commercial litigation, before he joined us. (Our sister chose not to enter the family business. She and her husband run a successful landscaping and daylily business.)

Family involvement didn't end with my generation. We had fourth-generation leaders in the business as well. My brother's son was a territory manager and regional sales manager. My son worked in human resources and safety and as a part-time floor supervisor. They had both joined us as their first full-time jobs. They were the next generation of potential leaders for the business. Their readiness, desires, and connection to the business were traits that would be assessed as they participated in the business to determine their ability and willingness to lead the business.

(Incidentally, the business was always presented to family members as an opportunity and not a directive for participation. All third- and fourth-generation workers had spent time on the production floor learning how to be a contributing team player in that process. As they matured, they were elevated within the business to higher levels of responsibility.)

Beyond the family, we had developed a leadership team that could take the business to the next level. We had selected professional, committed individuals in all facets of the business: sales, accounting, operations, transportation, factory management, purchasing, and customer service. They were the core of the business and responsible for its success.

My grandfather, my father, and my uncle left that earlier business and started their own company to grow. It went on to become a successful family business, providing us with a very comfortable living and purposeful work. Now, it was our turn to determine its future.

The Why

Our family had built a successful business. We were known to provide superior service and product to our clients. Our commitment to marketing, sales, service, and retail training was second to none. We had grown the business into an independent super-regional producer, one of the few that existed outside the top-tier producers. We had developed relationships with our vendors, and we were sought after as a customer. Our team contained the best people and enjoyed a progressive, supportive working environment. The family loved our business. It had provided good lives for our team and had afforded many team members comfortable retirements.

💬 *Our family had built a successful business.*

Our family had served in many positions within our industry's association, giving back to the industry that had provided for us. Our grandfather had served as president of that association for a period. We had all served or participated on the industry's flagship association and its various committees and causes.

We had kept a low profile in the community over the years, but we paid back the community by providing help for needy children and families in the local school system. If we heard about a family who had lost their home to a disaster, we donated product for them to resume their lives as normally as possible.

So why sell? Our business had wavered up and down on the acceptable profitability scale for more than 20 years as we searched for the right combination of product, sales, growth, and profitability to sustain the business for the benefit of our stakeholders. We had made acquisitions that proved to be ill-planned fits and ended up costing us more than we paid. Our business customers were being consolidated into larger entities, could not compete in the changed marketplace, and were fading away as their owners retired, died, or failed to plan for leadership succession. Other regional and small manufacturers were being consolidated into larger operations or were falling to the stresses of the Great Recession. Then new online marketers and direct-to-consumer operations entered the market and further divided our piece of the pie, turning it into slivers not slices. The top competitors in our space had market share of more than 66 percent, which didn't leave much room for the remaining businesses.

My grandfather coined a phrase that my father and uncle repeated to us: "I cannot believe how hard you have to work to make a sale!" I echoed this same statement to our fourth generation in the same way. The pace of the business was intensifying and getting faster every year. Each decision was becoming more critical than the last based on the changes in our customers and our competitors.

💬 *"I cannot believe how hard you have to work to make a sale!"*

You may have seen the poker tournaments on ESPN where the gamblers go all-in with their chips, taking the calculated risk that they will win. That was us. The family had placed its entire net worth in the business and signed off on loan guarantees greater than that amount to keep the business going. We describe ourselves as an "all-in" family.

Business Lineage

I had become CEO in 2008 while continuing my duties as vice president of operations. My brother was president of sales and marketing, and my youngest brother was chief financial officer. All of us had worn many hats in our careers within the business and had become schooled in the intricacies of it.

⊙ *We were doing business as we always had.*

By 2011, three years into my tenure as CEO, it was business as usual. We were doing business as we always had. Did you catch that "always"? We were under the delusion that the business model we had followed was going to keep serving us as it had in the past. We were on a revenue and profit roller-coaster, and I was getting very unsettled about the direction of the business and the pace at which we were moving. We didn't want to examine our thinking about the business because what we were doing had always delivered comfortable results.

My youngest brother has said, "I hate introspection; it's painful." How true! We didn't want to look at ourselves with fresh eyes because it hurt. Why? Because we couldn't see how the business should change so that it would yield better results and meet our expectations as family owners. Our attitude wasn't one of constantly looking at how we could improve; that took too much effort and change. We didn't believe it to be worth the effort.

⊙ *"I hate introspection; it's painful."*

The problem with growth is that there is always some pain. Remember having "growing pains" as you were growing up? This same thing happens as businesses grow in revenue and profits. It also happens as team players in a business change their thinking about the business and how it makes a profit. And, believe it or not, change is painful to us as owners. When approached the right way, however, the result of all this change and pain is not all puppies and unicorns, but a focused, profit-producing, directed business, a business that offers its team a path to growth and development.

In 2011, I did a horrible thing, worthy of getting myself disinherited: I asked someone from outside our business to come and help us. I faced the truth that we weren't going in the direction that was best for our family and the business. We, as a family, always believed that we could do anything we needed to do — just give us enough runway to get it going. The reality was that the end of the runway was getting closer by the minute, and we wouldn't be able to take off if we didn't change our attitude, direction, and speed. We just didn't see how we needed to change. It was a tough sell to me and my brothers to accept the fact that we needed fresh eyes on the business. But those fresh eyes ended up being the best investment we'd ever made.

$\bigcirc$ *The end of the runway was getting closer by the minute.*

We engaged with Lewis Rudy, whom I had met through the recommendation of a trusted, mutual business acquaintance. Lewis seemed the right fit for us. He had run his own family business, sold it, and worked for the purchaser for several years, eventually running that company. He had moved into the consulting space and had been practicing for several years when I met with him. Lewis developed and taught the MORE™ process of business re-engineering to meet the expectations of the owners of the business. The MORE™ re-engineering of our business not only made our business better, it created value in the business itself. It was a long, hard journey that had a great ending.

We weren't sure where the MORE™ process would take us, but we knew one thing: it would help us develop our business so we would have options for the business and ourselves. When we engaged Lewis, we felt we only had one option: run the business until we exited. We were so deeply entrenched in the day-to-day operations of the business that, if one of us were not able to participate in the business, it would cause the business to stumble or falter. We didn't feel we could sell the business, transition it to the next generation, or grow it appreciably. MORE™ gave us a clearer view of all the options available to us and the potential impact on the business and ourselves.

> ⌕ *We felt we only had one option. MORE™ gave us a clearer view of all the options.*

The end result was that we sold our business to a well-qualified family business in December of 2016. It was the best possible situation for the family to receive the maximum value for the business. We were equipped as a plug-and-play business. Management was in place to run the business, and processes had been implemented to ensure sustainability of the day-to-day operations and reporting. We had restructured the business to create maximum value by being able to remove ourselves, the owners, from day-to-day operations.

The timeline for the purchase process ran from first contact with the eventual buyer in November 2015 until the December 2016 closing. It was a long and arduous slog. Yes, a slog. It was painful, excruciating, humbling, frustrating, embarrassing, and just about every other dreadful emotional word. My youngest brother and I discussed on numerous occasions how we had never worked this hard at this pace for this duration of time — and we had worked hard on our business. In the end, however, it was worth everything we endured.

The purchase secured the continuity of the business and placed the family in a better financial position. All three brothers exited the business on our own terms.

CHAPTER 2
Value Creation

Business value is not achieved easily. It took five years, from 2011 through 2015, for us to move our business from an owner-dependent business, where we provided the lion's share of the value, to a business using professional management that could create value with minimal owner involvement. I hired the operations manager who replaced me in October 2015, the month before we received a phone call of interest from our buyer and 14 months before we sold the business. The purchaser asked me, before all other personnel decisions had been made, who was going to take my place and run the operation. I had an answer! I had planned for this. I was expendable, which was a highly-satisfying feeling. Does this seem like a reasonable statement to you? If not, why?

> ⊙ *I was expendable, which was a highly satisfying feeling.*

From 2011 to 2015, we had reverse-engineered our business from what it was to what it should be, to what we planned for it to be to produce maximum value. The path and process we followed is the Master of Reverse Engineering (MORE™) process.

💬 It took five years.

The process was not easy. We had to untie 47 years of family business history and processes. We had to break habits we all had and develop new ones. We had to change, which is the hardest thing a person can do. We all take change personally, as well we should. However, when change is necessary to produce a better outcome, you must swallow your pride and work together to make it better.

Our team engaged in MORE™ and at the same time continued managing the business on a day-to-day basis. Our marketplace and customer base rapidly evolved. Suppliers consolidated to the point that it inhibited our ability to source. We had an escalating need for more professional production management. Quality labor supply was slim and disappearing at a rapid rate, changing almost overnight. Our competitors had consolidated into large entities, giving them the advantages of scale and distribution. Our costs were always under pressure from all sides in all areas. And the pace of business was getting faster and faster. How were we going to adapt, change, overcome, and survive in this environment? Our challenge was to manage the change of how we were going to conduct business, while we were engaged in the day-to-day activities of the business.

💬 We had built silos. Got silos?

Like many organizations, we had built silos with walls of solid steel around ourselves, our processes, and our functional units so the forces of change couldn't penetrate the defenses. We were constantly on point with heightened senses to any attack predicated on who we were and how we did our jobs.

Silos are just what they sound like. They have walls and a roof, and there is one way in and one way out. Generally, they are used in farming to store grain products until they are sold at market. The farmer controls what goes in and what goes out. In the same way, a business can have silos, self-contained units with walls and a roof manufactured by the leader of the functional area, whether that's the operations manager, chief financial officer, sales manager, chief information officer, or department supervisor. They determine what goes in and what comes out, serving as the keepers of the goods, so to speak. The problem is that they operate like small fiefdoms where their princes control communication, projects, and other value-adding operations. And they do not share well. The synergies that are usually enjoyed by businesses with transparent and open communication and sharing of resources are the ones likely to thrive and grow. Silos were detrimental to the goals we had set for the business in the greatest way. Each functional area kept to itself. The unspoken motto was "All for none, and none for all."

In many other ways, we were a typical family business. The description of our business is not unlike yours. As we go through the MORE™ process of creating value in your business, I will use other examples of my business and examples from Lewis Rudy, our trusted advisor and author of the MORE™ process, to which you will be able to relate.

CHAPTER 3
Give Me MORE™!

MORE™: Master of Reverse Engineering

This part of our journey together will be an overview of MORE™, the process of reverse engineering your business to create value for you, the owner. If that does not sound very enjoyable, or if you are hesitant about changing the status quo because your business is doing okay, then you are in the right place.

The MORE™ process has been successfully implemented in businesses of all types and sizes. It has universal application in manufacturing businesses. It has resulted in large performance gains in people, processes, and, best of all, profits. At its root, MORE™ is a process that uncovers constraints within the business and helps the owner and his team develop plans to change the way the business behaves. Constraints are present in people, processes, culture, and thinking about the purpose and direction of the business. They are in every nook and cranny of the business.

💬 *Change the way the business behaves.*

MORE™ is a holistic approach to building business value. Every aspect of your business is tied together. You cannot change one aspect of your business without affecting the other parts of your business; it's a disservice to try to fix just one part. One single change can ripple through your entire business. MORE™ understands this vital fact and anticipates cascading changes across the entire business.

MORE™ asks hard questions about people, the core asset of every business. I cannot overemphasize the importance of having the right people on the trip with you. People are the key to producing profit, not the product you sell or the service you offer. Making sure you have the right people on board is worth the time and money spent. This is not an easy thing to do. You should give great care and consideration to the people you hire. They will become a part of your business, culture, and life. Does that put perspective on their importance?

Willingness to forget what has been done and to move forward in a new and uncomfortable direction is key in the MORE™ process. It all begins with you, the business owner. You must engage in the process and lead the change in your business. It was very hard for me to pull back from the exciting adrenaline rush of the whirlwind of daily operations. The whirlwind is addictive.

I remember the first time I became aware of the changes taking place in our business. We were moving a piece of equipment in the factory, and I was out on the floor pushing and pulling with everyone else to get the machine into a new home. Just so you understand, I had a personal connection with this machine. I had bought it, installed it, and run it for months until we found an operator. It was my baby. As I was "helping," the others all looked at me and said, "You need to stop and do something else. We have this." Talk about a slap in the face to wake you up! They realized more than I that we were changing and that I had more important things to do to help them than moving a machine. I needed to work on the business and not in the business. That is what MORE™ is all about. You are not the value of the business; you are adding value to it.

Creating a Gap

As a businessperson, you've probably been taught to look for and eliminate gaps. By doing an assessment of the business and identifying its strengths, weaknesses, opportunities, and threats (SWOT), you can identify the gaps that exist between the current state to the expected state. These gaps are then filled with action plans to move the business from the current state to the expected state. Under normal circumstances, plans are made to close a gap, moving the current state of a process, action, or team member to the desired state.

With MORE™, however, we actually want to create and widen a specific gap. We want to create a gap of value in the business itself, where the desired state is you being less involved on a daily basis. We want the dependence on the owners to create value minimized. We want the owners to move away from the day-to-day activities of the business. This is what I mean about working on the business and not in the business. You need to create white space so you can focus on how the business and its people, physical assets, and business processes create value. As you step out of the daily whirlwind of operations, the business becomes more valuable on the basis that it's creating value, profit, growth, or any other metric you wish to track.

💬 *The desired state is you being less involved on a daily basis.*

Staying Away

Still not convinced? Ask yourself this simple question, "How long can I be away from the business before it begins to move from its expected focus?" One year, one month, one week, or maybe one day? I remember the days when we shut down for vacations. We did not have any room for the business to lose focus, so all of us went on holiday at the same time. (We were lucky to take off national holidays and not disappoint our customers.)

Shutting down your business for one or two weeks is not realistic in today's fast-moving marketplace. Does the business still push for change and growth while you are away, or does it coast along? What does your answer say about your business? What does your answer say about the value you are bringing to the business? I know we all want to be important and needed in our business. I was that way. I would come into the building on some days and have 10 or more people waiting on me for answers or decisions. That really made me feel valuable and needed. It's a great feeling to be needed. But when you are needed, *you* are the value, instead of the *business* being the value. And that lowers the value of the business.

Add Value; Don't Be the Value

I thought I was adding value to the business by being the go-to guy for all the questions. In fact, I wasn't allowing the business to create value. If you, Mr. or Ms. Owner, are doing what I did, you are the value in the business. This is a serious dysfunction. You must add value to your business, not be the value in your business. Otherwise, when you exit your business — and we all will do that one way or the other — the business will start beginning its exit also — unless you have a plan.

💬 *You must add value to your business, not be the value in your business.*

You might say the same thing I said: "Plan?" How can I plan when I am so busy every day getting orders out, answering a gazillion questions, and doing work for my reports so they can do their work? "I am the only one who does that, you think. I can do it faster and better so I will do it, you believe. Do you see what is wrong with this picture? The business needs your attention; it deserves your attention. There is only one person with the view from the top like yours, and that is what is most important to your business.

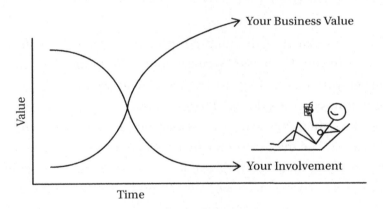

People, People, People

Here is where you create the most value: investing time in your people so they can fully realize their potential. People drive the business forward under your direction, vision, and guidance. All the technologies, automation, computer systems, and processes we employ in our businesses are just tools for our people to do their jobs in the most effective and productive manner. People make the decisions and actions that move your business forward. Businesses are people.

The right people doing the right things at the right times: that is the magic of business. Peter Drucker said, "Get the right things done." More simple and profound words have never been uttered. It's the right people who get the right things done. Have the courage to surround yourself with people who are more competent, better qualified, and more successful than you. Building a great team of people will rocket your business forward. Build that superstar team and hold on for the ride of your life!

> *Have the courage to surround yourself with people who are more competent, better qualified, and more successful than you.*

Do you see how creating this high-performance team will create more value in your business? What are your expectations for your people and your team? How are they being held accountable for the right things they are doing? The less your people rely on you to know the right things to do, the greater the value you create in your business. The measure of the business's reliance on you is one gap metric you want as low as possible. I had to work intentionally and purposely to drive this down. When I was asked my opinion, I learned to ask, "How are you going to do it?" before I ever made a comment. Try it; it's amazing to see how creative the approaches to problems become. Do it, and you will see the value of your business increase over time.

Will you make hires that don't fit or work well? You can be sure of it. In those cases, as soon as you know there are issues, let the appropriate person, their direct report, investigate and have a conversation with them about the issues. Then develop an agreed-upon plan to change the behavior. (Yes, it's a behavior, not an issue.) The point is that all our actions have consequences and when the consequences of our actions run contrary to the values, direction, and purpose of the business, those actions/behaviors must change. Ignoring the behavior and hoping it will change is not a successful business strategy. Hope is never a strategy. Deal directly, authentically, and truthfully with people, and you will be paid back in improved performance and profits. If the behavior continues, there must be a defined, communicated process of escalating consequences for failure to change.

MORE™ Process Outline

Below is a short outline of the MORE™ process. The full process involves many in-between steps and is not the same for every business. Your business will have its own nuances to address and consider at each step.

1. Interview with Ownership

2. Gather Information About the Business

3. Develop a Strengths, Weaknesses, Opportunities, and Threats (SWOT) Analysis for the Business

4. Develop a Gap Report for the Business

5. Vision, Mission, Values, and Goals

6. Review the Interviews, SWOT Analysis, and Gap Analysis with Ownership

7. Kickoff Meeting with Key Team Members

8. Core MORE™ Concepts the Business Must Embrace

9. Development of Strategic Plans

10. Succession and Transition Plans

The initial processes up to the development of the strategic plans will take about 60 to 90 days, depending on the circumstances of your business. The rest of the process is dependent on the scalability, culture, and people within the business. In our experience, it takes at least a year of face-to-face conversations to make appreciable impact in the day-to-day perception of you and your key team members. Old thinking and habits die hard. It takes time to change the way a business and its people act, lead, and manage.

In chapters 4 through 13, I will go into more detail about the MORE™ system and describe the steps and processes within the steps. MORE™ involves you and your team. It takes your time, leadership, and commitment to be successful. It's hard work and demands consistent effort. The time expended involves both learning to think about the business differently and changing to meet the expectations of the re-engineered business. Based on my experience, it's time well spent!

CHAPTER 4
Interview with Ownership

The first step of the MORE™ process is an interview conducted by your MORE™ advisor with you, the owner of the business. This is a conversation about your business and how it's doing. You realize this is a loaded question. How is it doing? In what respect? At what time? The other question involves understanding why you want to talk to someone you barely know about a very personal and sensitive subject, your business. What do you want your business to achieve? You must have a great deal of discomfort or outright pain about the lack of performance of your business. The business does not seem right. Do you feel it? This meeting defines what is troubling you about the business.

The questions involved are personal and probing. You would typically not ask yourself these questions because they force you to go to uncomfortable places. You need someone to guide you to realize and communicate the true state of your business; I know I did.

You will also describe the financial and organizational condition of the business. Another important discussion concerns your team. Describing the people in your business is very important. They are who will make the strategic plans and execute them per your instructions. They must be engaged and have full buy-in to the plans or nothing will happen. They must be capable and willing to live the mission and values of your business every day. They must be willing and prepared to call out others that miss the mark and bring them back onto the path.

⏺ *A Conversation with You, the Owner*

Your team and their participation is not optional. They are the largest key to success and your greatest asset. If they cannot align themselves with the mission, values, and goals of the business, their influence will spread through your business and destroy what you are working to accomplish. Sometimes they are not a fit for where the business is going and need to seek another place to ply their trade. If this does not happen, they will hinder everyone's progress and growth.

In one business we know of, the production team leaders resisted the changes that needed to be made to increase the production to match the sales rate that had been forecast. This negativity and inaction had a detrimental effect on the entire production team. It became glaringly obvious when they couldn't make the forecast production demand. The business lost the confidence of their customers and they lost revenue — that was given to other vendors. It took years to regain their customers' confidence. Everyone on the leadership team must be on board. There can be no exceptions. The stakes are too high.

Establishing What the Owner Wants to Change and Why

I remember talking with Lewis Rudy about what led me to reach out to him. I told Lewis a mutual business acquaintance had suggested a call with him would be beneficial. He understood that, then asked, "Why did you call me?" The answer to this question was uncomfortable, embarrassing, and painful for me to verbalize, but it framed the rest of our five-year journey together. I spilled my guts. I told him that I was quite uncomfortable with the direction and growth of our business. We kept doing the same things, in the same way over and over, and we expected to get better results. Albert Einstein defined insanity as doing the same thing over and over again and expecting different results. He was way smarter than I am on many levels.

The second reason I gave Lewis was that I was not getting any younger and stayed awake at night wondering how our owners were going to exit the business. We didn't know how much we expected to receive from a sale, and so we couldn't live a particular lifestyle or have a transition plan with options in place. It wasn't happening. A buyer didn't stumble upon us to find we were magically ready. It took a plan and five years to move the business.

How about you? Do you have a plan to exit your business other than dying in your chair? What happens if you are disabled and unable to work or incompetent to make business decisions? This last statement can be your family's worst nightmare. You owe it to your family and your business to plan for transition. However, if your business is not operating on its own and on all eight cylinders, what, if anything, is really of value to transition?

We were creating enough gross profit to pay ourselves and live a comfortable life. We were not profitable enough to pay ourselves and pay our stockholders (the three owners) a return on their investment. This was a big issue to me. We would have made more return on our investment by putting our family money into stocks. We had become complacent and numb to the idea of return on investment. More should be gained from the business than just making a comfortable living. We settled for the comfortable lifestyle for many years.

Establishing Agreed–Upon Deliverables

I met with Lewis a couple of times before I nailed down what I wanted the engagement to deliver for the business and us, the owners. The outcome of the meetings, besides engaging Lewis to work with us, was a set of goals and expectations for the business that we would work on together to create value. These goals would ensure that we not only would grow but that we would flourish. The goals of the business may be stated in different ways, but they all relate to the goals of creating expected profitability and value in the business.

Profitability

This is the most important metric of your business. A business cannot grow and develop on marginal profitability. Does your profitability look and feel like valleys and peaks? Perhaps the business produces outstanding or acceptable profit one year and then — hang on — free falls to the bottom. The market has changed, unplanned expenses balloon, vendors have price increases, and you have not planned for any of these. This is not good for the business, your team, or you, as the owner. It stresses your team and the business. Operating under stress never produces optimal performance. Graph your profits; what do they look like over a 10- or 20-year period?

Profit should be built into the budget from the bottom line up. It's the goal and number to be met. Profit should not be the least planned item on the profit-and-loss statement. It is the planned item. All the other expense and income items are derived after profit is identified and put into the plan. Profit is non-negotiable for a growing, flourishing business.

Adopting this process necessitated a change in our thinking about the business. Historically, we had taken the prior t year's revenue and added a percentage for growth. We had then applied historical percentages to all expense and income categories and magically at the bottom of the budget, the number we would settle for called profit would appear. "Settle" is the key word here. We didn't look at the budget categories and have a strategic plan for each that would yield us a defined profit we wanted from the business.

MORE™ does the opposite. It defines the profit that is expected for the business and its stakeholders and develops strategic plans in all areas to produce that profit. Do not settle for a profit. Grow it and think differently about all aspects of your business and how all changes internally and externally are opportunities to increase your profit. Work from the bottom line up, profit, being a fixed item.

Settling for something is never productive. Have you seen how dirt settles when you fill in a hole? You must overfill the hole with dirt, so when it settles, it is level with the ground. In the same way, you must overfill profit so when the dust settles at the end of the year it is level with your expectation. Events happen, and you must keep alert to messages that are sent from all corners of your business. Then act on those messages, plan how to correct or capitalize, and protect your profit. You are the gatekeeper, and you can control your profit. It takes vigilance and planning. A MORE™ company never settles; it's always growing and improving. Constantly improving the business is the conversation of the business.

In our business, we found that our delivery drivers were a wealth of information about our customers. One day, a driver casually mentioned that he saw a competitor's truck delivering to a customer at the same time as him. However, this customer was not buying from our competitor. This immediately sent us on a mission to find out why this event had happened and what we needed to do to increase his business and consequently ours. It turned out that our customer was looking for additional product to lengthen his line. Guess what? We had what he was looking for; so we made the sale, increased his and our revenue, and increased his and our profit. Messages come from all places in your business; you must listen intently.

A MORE™ company takes the desired plan, looks at the business and re-engineers the business to realize the expected profit. No stones are left unturned to understand the expenses and revenues. Every aspect of the business is laid open and examined. An intense questioning of each area is applied. How is _____ performing? How should _____ perform? Fill in the blank for every area of your business. Measurement of key metrics in these areas before, during, and after the process is the key to gauging the success of your plans and actions. This is an ongoing process that never stops or stalls in a MORE™ company.

Value Creation

What is business value? Book value? Market value? Customer value? As in all things, a business is worth what someone else is willing to pay for it, not what you think it is worth. I repeat: your idea of the value of the business is not relevant here under any succession or transition plan. In your eyes, the business is your blood, sweat, and tears over many years. Unfortunately, you do not get paid for that assessment. You get paid for the business's value to someone else.

Whether it's by venture capital, a strategic buyer, an insider buying the business, or a family successor, you get paid for the value you create in your business. If you are a large part of the value, then the whole worth of the business includes you. If your goal is to back out of the business or reduce the number of hours you participate in the business, you will have a different set of business values and options to consider that will not be to your liking.

I left our business by choice the day we closed our transaction. If you are integral to the business, you will not have that choice; leaving will not be an option, at least for a considerable period. Staying in the business after someone else has control after years of making decisions and doing it your way is difficult at best. My brothers left three months after I did. Their frustration grew each day they remained past the close of the transaction. They were not able to do things their way. Our buyers were as good as they get, but they had their own agenda, goals, and way of doing business.

Value is created and measured in a business in several ways. First and foremost, is the free cash flow from operations. A simple definition of cash flow is the total amount of money being transferred into and out of a business, especially as it affects liquidity. Cash flow is a prime indicator of the health of the business and directly reflects the liquidity of the business. Cash flow indicates how well the business can pay its vendors, pay its employees, fund capital expenditures, pay down debt, collect its receivables, and pay a return to its stockholders.

Free cash flow is cash flow less capital expenditures necessary to maintain the business's assets. This is what is left over and theoretically available to the stockholders if the business does not choose to spend it on growth. Simply put, free cash flow is available to the stockholders to commit to growth, investment in the business, or distribution to the stockholders. The greater your free cash flow, the greater the value of the business.

Value is created by the profits the business generates from operations. The greater your profits, the greater the value of your business. Accurate and timely financials are essential to success in this realm. Many companies use an outside CPA firm to perform a yearly audit. This is a great way to show anyone outside your business that your financials represent a fair and true picture of your business's health. Another goal to set is to have a five-day close at the end of an accounting period. Any longer, and you are looking at ancient history as the basis for measuring your results and making course-correction plans.

Value is created through your team. People execute the plans and actions that generate profit for your business. If your team doesn't know, understand, or care what your goals are, they won't contribute to the success of the business. If they aren't properly prepared and educated on key issues such as how the business makes a sale, how the business makes profit, or what profit the business needs to support itself, likely your business will miss out on the opportunity to be highly successful. A good team needs attention from you, their leader, to achieve their full potential. You must engage, encourage, and energize them.

At a minimum, the time on the ground with your business is a period of one year. After that year, a mutual reevaluation of the relationship and how it needs to proceed must be done. It's up to you to decide whether the work continues as-is or if it's time to change the relationship. The relationship change can take multiple forms as long as there is agreement on both sides. The goal of MORE™ is for you to be successful; there is nothing else that takes precedence over your and the business's success.

CHAPTER 5

Gather Information About the Business

Prepare Your Team to Meet Your Goals and Expectations

Now begins the work and excitement of finding out the current state of your business and what it will take to meet your goals and expectations. You have set your goals and expectations for the business, your team, and yourself. The next step for a MORE™ company is to make plans to exceed your goals and expectations. This may seem to be an easy exercise, but it's where everything you hold sacred in your business is challenged.

I can hear your questions: "Lee, why are we changing this aspect of our business? It's doing fine" and "We have always done it that way. Why change?" These philosophies lead to a slow and lingering death of your business. You will be asked these questions and more. Be prepared to answer consistently and honestly. If an aspect of the business is not performing, address it.

Do not sidestep the questions; meet them head on, challenge them, and make your business better. This means processes, people, customers, marketing, logistics, materials, anything that is not performing in a way to meet your goals as a business.

Step up and challenge the sacred cows of the business. Your personal favorites should be first on the examination table. Deconstruct them with your team and see how they can be reconstructed to improve the business and move the business toward its goals. Everyone will have processes and people that are performing fine. "Fine" is not a great word. When you ask your significant other how your relationship is going and they say, "fine," what do you feel? It's the same way with an aspect of your business that is performing fine. Our first reaction is to say if it's not broken don't fix it. MORE™ says that if it's not contributing as expected to the goals of the business, break it and re-engineer in its place a better solution that improves the business and moves it to its goals.

Do not take breaking and re-engineering lightly. Make sure you understand the process or person under examination correctly. Ask your team to contribute to this examination. Decide after carefully examining the after-effects of the decision.

One-on-One interviews of Key Personnel

A great starting place for your team is to understand the personalities of your key team members and how they communicate with each other. This can be done by using a four-quadrant personality profile test.

There are many types of personality assessment tests. I prefer the DISC® tool, which measures dominance, influence, steadiness, and conscientiousness. It's easy to understand and gives you information on how to communicate and work with a person given your own personality and communication style. This is an online test that shows how your team members are likely to communicate, make decisions, and behave under differing circumstances. It generates a graphic representation of the four basic personalities in comparison to the others, which makes it easy for each team member to grasp how they are likely to communicate and how they can more effectively communicate with each other.

As leaders, our job is to help our teams be successful. The personality assessment will also show where people may struggle making decisions when they are under pressure. Our job is to recognize when they are struggling and develop a plan to constructively help them move through the tough decisions they will face. We must work with them to be successes in their own space. Success increases their confidence and broadens their thinking about the possibilities of the business.

More information about this test online and in written form is available for you to explore. In essence, each person is given the link to take the DISC assessment, which will take 15 to 20 minutes. Then they will receive their results, as will you. Once each team member has taken the test, the tests will be accumulated to produce a team profile. This is a great tool to open communication and make your team aware of how they might be perceived by their fellow team members and you. Business is best done as a team. The synergies derived from the meshing of different skill sets and viewpoints is exciting and can be very productive. You must manage the interplay of your team members. The DISC gives you a great tool to see your team.

After the DISC personality assessment tests are taken, you will schedule a series of one-on-one, no-holds-barred, uncensored meetings with your key team members you've identified and any other team members you feel are relevant. People to consider are your top-level managers, family members and relatives working in the business, relevant stockholders, and important shareholders.

Each interview is confidential and between your team member and your MORE™ advisor. Your team members will reveal more about your business than you want to hear. They have been holding back in fear that they will offend you. This interview with a third party gives a voice to your team. You will learn about their view of where your business is, what is holding it back, and where it can go. You will get an accurate picture of the business from their input. Remember that your view of the business is not their view of the business. They are dependent on the business for their livelihood and will have views of your and the team's performance that create a picture of how the business acts and reacts.

⊙ *They have been holding back in fear.*

The interview starts with a blank page, and notes are written down as your team member speaks. It's a fear-free environment that produces open dialog about your business. Questions are asked about you — yes, you. How is the business going? What role do they play in the business? What needs to be changed to be successful? What does success look like for this business? Other relevant questions are also asked as needed to understand the business and its performance constraints and practices. These results in aggregate will be shared with you and your team, but the comments will not be identifiable as to who said them. That is critically important. Anonymity creates a safe environment and atmosphere so the information can be shared without issue. When the interview process is done correctly, it highlights the effects of increased material costs, ineffective labor, and other real costs to your business. This is not easily revealed unless your team members are properly interviewed and feel free to discuss the state of your business.

These interviews are designed to not lead or direct the team members in any direction; they're designed to draw out their honest and open feedback about the business and their role in the business. They will take the conversation in the way they desire. (I must say I got a sinking feeling in the pit of my stomach when I realized the license we had given our team members and when I heard what they had to say.)

The information revealed in these interviews is impressive. If you think your people are open with you, think again. I found that even the closest, most involved, trusted team members were still holding back from speaking their minds openly. Whether it's fear of reprisal, fear of rejection, or fear of hurting you or someone else, the result is that you have not seen what they see as they see it. The information obtained has always been there. It takes a fresh set of eyes and an open environment to bring it out. Do not feel as if this is your fault. You have had an open-door policy, encouraged detrimental and constructive comments, and been their coach, mentor, and advisor. But you are their boss, and you own the business. Those two facts are enough to intimidate and shut down the flow of communication, regardless of your efforts to encourage open dialogue with your team.

The common threads in the interviews are not new news to the team or you because you have already seen them and they already know them. Seeing them as a team in print gives the feedback teeth. Suddenly, you and your team are sharing real, detailed information in real time.

Financial Assessment of the Business

While the interview process is taking place, you will be asked to produce documents pertaining to the financial state of the business. These are needed to ascertain how to meet the financial and growth goals of the business. Detailed profit-and-loss statements for the last five years, current profit-and-loss, customer list with sales and sales concentration, products or services sold and their concentrations, cash flow statement, and current budget and comparison to actual are among the documents needed to focus on growing the profitability of the business. These documents may or may not exist, so a discussion around how to get the information is critical.

Sharing these documents was a big deal for us. We had never shared our financials outside the senior management team, so giving them to a person outside the business was a big step. This decision didn't come with any small amount of discussion. The thought of someone reading our "report card" for the business for the past five years was scary. Why? It made me realize that what we had done and the results we had generated would be scrutinized and, frankly, we were not proud of our results. Fortunately, I got over it. The pain of sharing and hearing objective judgment was less than the pain of not moving the business as fast or as profitably as was needed.

The financial goals that are set with the owner are the top-level key metrics from which success will be measured. Businesses require a profit to stay healthy, provide jobs, and deliver a return to their investors. Profit must come first! When pricing your product or service, start at the bottom and put profit on the bottom line and build up. The parts of your financial statement between revenue and profit must be managed to produce the desired profit goal. Then work up to what you can deliver for the price and profit the business deserves.

💬 *"We hope we are profitable this year" is not a strategy or a plan.*

It's not uncommon to see that profit is the result of sales minus everything else. It's a leftover. "We hope we are profitable this year" is not a strategy or a plan. Profit should and can be managed. Managing profitability is exactly what you do when you work on the business and not in the business. When you manage your business in this way, it will produce value in itself and by itself. Each line on the income statement should have an owner who is responsible for the expected goal for that line. They are responsible for developing strategic plans to reach the desired expectation. When all the lines of the income statement are managed in this process, the bottom line is produced, not just a leftover.

Organizational Assessment of the Business

Next, comes an organizational assessment, which means more than looking at an organizational chart and seeing that all the positions are filled. This is a multi-level subject that will be peeled back like an onion.

The outside layer is your current organizational chart and how it flows. Do you have job descriptions and descriptive metric expectations that workers know about? Do you have all the current team positions filled to be successful in your day-to-day operations? What are they doing? What is the focus of their job? Are they doing activities that take them away from maximizing their unique contributions to the business? Are they performing productively and executing in a timely manner? Are they the right people for the jobs they are doing? What is their bandwidth? All these questions and more must be answered to gain a full understanding of the team and to maximize its working structure.

The inner layer involves identifying the key team members who will lead your business to success. They are identified by their high productivity and extensive knowledge of your business. Team members holding key positions are also feeders of information and action-oriented. "Let's get something done" is their mantra. They make the business flow and run daily. This is not you! Remember, you are not the value of your business; your team is. You are important, and your value is added by working on the business and not in the business. Prepare yourself for the hard questions in this layer that question the ability of the current team to transition to the vision and future of your business.

The next inner layer looks at your business in several potential future states. The prerequisite for this is a vision of where you want to go and a strategic plan of how you are going to get there. You must see into your future and align your team over time to that vision. From the vision and the strategic plan, you must project the team member positions that it will take to grow and meet your goals. Along with these positions, you must define what they are doing and how their contribution to the goal is measured. You don't want to add people for the sake of adding. Each position must be carefully assessed.

⌕ *Your business is the people in your business.*

Another reminder about people. Your business is the people in your business. Everyone in your organization must be the right person for the position, not a placeholder. You need true team members. If they are not productive, if they do not work with your team, if they are solitary players, or for any reason do not fit the business, they will not work in your business or for that matter, likely in most businesses. You do not need them. As painful as that statement is, I have witnessed firsthand how one person can derail your business just when it's gaining momentum and moving at 110 miles per hour. It creates a horrible mess when it crashes.

The other side is that you must be compassionate to all team members. Everyone deserves humane and ethical treatments no matter how egregiously they have acted or behaved toward you or the business. This is one of the hardest aspects of servant leadership. You are not serving or teaching your errant team member as a leader if they are not apprised of exactly how they are not living up to their expectations as a member on your team. A separation from your business should not be a surprise to any team member. The exceptions should be few and far between. Hire carefully, my friend; be quick to evaluate, coach, reprimand, and finally, if necessary, to help them move on to a better place.

CHAPTER 6
Develop a Strengths, Weaknesses, Opportunities, and Threats (SWOT) Analysis for the Business

Doing an assessment of strengths, weaknesses, opportunities, and threats is the beginning of the formation of the strategic plans of the business. The SWOT document is presented by aggregating the information from the DISC tests, interviews, financial review, and your expectations and goals for the business. The first draft of this presentation is for you to review and give your feedback. The next draft is for presentation to the key team members during a facilitated kickoff meeting.

During the interviews, common core issues will be revealed that are causing the symptoms of nonperformance in the business. When your team members can speak freely, without you present, the amount of valuable insights about your business that will come out is uncanny.

Current thinking about the elements of a SWOT report is that the first two parts, strengths and weaknesses, typically have internal causes, while the second two pieces, opportunities and threats, have external causes acting upon the business. A MORE™ business will recognize that opportunities and threats will also originate from inside the business. Proprietary product innovation and specialized skill sets that produce revenue for the business are examples of opportunities that can arise from within the business. The death or disabling of a key team member or the death or disabling of the owner are extreme examples of internally-generated threats to the business.

⬭ We reflect, plan, and act on circumstances.

This is a key thought process of a MORE™ business. If you think that circumstances or the whims of customers dictate the direction of your business, they probably will. A MORE™ business believes that we reflect, plan, and act on circumstances that come from both inside and outside of our business. Instead of just saying, "It is what it is," add "But it will be what we make it." That addition gives you power to move the business forward. Don't become disillusioned and dejected because the world around you changes. Make something happen. As Bob Dylan sang, "The Times They Are a-Changin'." News flash: they will always be a-changin'. This is the thrill and excitement of running your business. Make the most of the change, think about it, and turn change into an opportunity for your business to grow.

The SWOT report will identify key issues in the following areas that need change to produce value in the business:

- Leadership
- Revenue sources
- Sales process and management
- Marketing
- Operations

- Purchasing

- Finance

- Human resources and talent acquisition

- Product innovation

- Organizational components

- Deliverables

- Goal Setting

These key areas are reviewed as to their efficiency and productivity. It's vitally important that all areas of the business are operating at peak to produce a healthy, flourishing business and to create value for the owners.

Strengths

The strengths of your business are what you excel at in the ordinary course of your business. This is normally thought of in the realm of customer interaction and fulfillment. Strengths of your business go beyond and gauge your business at every level: profit, cash flow, cash, innovation, marketing, brand, and team strength, as a few examples. These are the factors that will be built upon and leveraged to produce extraordinary results for your business. Build and develop the strengths of your business. Use them as leverage in your marketing and sales processes. What can you do that your competitors can't or won't? What is your value statement to your customers and prospects? What are the possibilities and opportunities that lie in your strengths? The strengths of your business hold untapped resources for improved revenue and profit.

Weaknesses

Weaknesses are the things you don't execute well. You will focus on these and develop plans to close the gap between what you expect to happen and what is currently happening. As you move ahead with your plan, you will move toward a position of strength. You will never, and I repeat never, be completely satisfied.

Your job as the leader of your business is to expect the best from everyone and everything in your business. Settling is not an option if you want to grow your business. Addressing the weaknesses of your business is all about action, urgency, and direction in narrowing the gap between reality and expectation.

Plans are essential for changing your weaknesses. Actions, deadlines, and accountability are the three essentials of a plan. Without a plan, you are not acknowledging that there is a weakness. If you do nothing, you will get the same results. If you work your plan, things will change. The plan is the roadmap to successfully changing your weakness into a strength.

Opportunities

Every day is filled with great opportunities for your business: the constant motion of the marketplace you are swimming in, the disruptions happening in the economy and marketplace, great and marketable innovations, and weaknesses in your competitors, just to name a few. What are the opportunities that currently exist for your business? Focus on how your glass is half full not half empty. What your competitors see as a problem you may be able to capitalize on to make revenue and profit. This portion of the SWOT analysis should be a great part of your focus in working on the business.

It's constantly changing and requires intentional attention to what is
happening to the environment of your business.

Threats

When has your business been threatened? Was it during the Great
Recession? Did your customers quit spending? Did your customer's customers stop buying? Do you have the talent on board to
execute and succeed in your goals and plans? Can you staff your core
manufacturing floor or creative pool? Are your material and labor
costs out of control? What does a nearly full employment rate or high
unemployment rate mean for your business? Are the channels of
distribution being disrupted and you are on the outside looking in?
Is your sales force delivering and growing expected revenue or are
they just taking orders? Most of these threats can be used as great
excuses for not growing or delivering on expectations. There is one
way to address these threats: choose not to participate. Plan, meet
them head on and deflect them around your business. But most
importantly never, never underestimate the impact they can have on
your business.

💬 *"The times they are a-changin'."*

The value of a SWOT report represents a picture of the reality of
your business and identifies the issues that need attention. It's not
a one-time event. Every year, I pulled our management team kicking
and screaming through the process, and at the end, we had a list of
actionable items. Then they would make and apply a strategic plan
to each one. This formed the basis of much of our reporting in our
management meetings since these actions would lead us to the
performance of the business we expected. Go forth and conquer!

CHAPTER 7

Develop a Gap Report for the Business

Where Are You Now?

Where is your business now? Where do you expect it to be? The gap report is a comparison of these two states of your business. This is the starting line from where you begin making strategic plans to bring the business to meet your expectations — not only your expectations but the expectations of your customers, team members, family owners, and the marketplace. It's easy to put the future or expected state at a low threshold to produce immediate results toward filling the gaps. The business deserves to have goals that challenge it and bring it into alignment with the marketplace. Setting the expectations too low, lacking specifics, or not having a realistic view of where your business is now is setting yourself up for failure. Both the starting line and the finish line must be determined realistically and accurately.

> *Where is your business now?*
> *Where do you expect it to be?*

Reality and accuracy create confidence in commitment. When you know the real condition of your business and that it has been accurately represented, you can plan the investment that your business is going to need to meet your goals and expectations. You will commit to investments in the currencies of capital, people, and your own most valuable currency, your time. This is going to be the ultimate investment in your business; remember you are all-in.

Do not fool yourself. I falsely believed we were in better shape than we were. In my mind, we were always in the right place, doing the right things, and making happy campers out of our team and customers. Take time to make a critical, honest analysis of where your business is performing currently.

Perhaps you are uncertain what you should measure. There are other key performance results that indicate the performance of your business besides profit. Ask yourself what the right things are that you should measure to ensure that your business is at peak profit and/or growth performance. Anything can be measured and tracked. It may take effort to determine how you measure soft costs and soft results, but you can do it if you put your mind to it.

⌕ *Anything can be measured and tracked.*

The most difficult thing that my business tried to quantify was the cost of turnover in our employee base. We had no idea what the impact of the loss of one employee was on our profit. There were many soft and incidental costs to consider. We worked on this for days to reveal all the costs. Our conclusion was astonishing. The cost of turnover per exiting employee was in the mid five-digit range in whole dollars. Once we identified this number, we put a strategic plan in place to reduce the amount of turnover in our business.

Where Do You Want to Be?

The other end of this equation determines where the business should be or is expected to be by its customers and owners. There are many places to gather this information. Trade associations are a wealth of knowledge. Owners of similar businesses can provide valuable insight. One really good source of comparison is roundtables. I was a fortunate to be a member of a CEO roundtable at our local chamber of commerce, and the connections and discussions around that table, pardon the pun, were invaluable. NAM, the National Association of Manufacturers, has great information on its website. Public relations and communication firms are another source. The Internet — the sum of the distillation of all human knowledge, as one of my friends describes it — has a wealth of information.

The Difference is the Gap

There are two different places you see your business when you determine the gap: the place where your business currently is on critical performance measures and the place where your business must be to meet your goals and expectations. The difference between your current state and your need-to state is the gap.

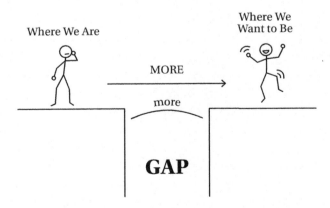

Moving the distance from current state to need-to state is hard work. It takes an all-in commitment to change from one state to the next. It requires committed quality time from you and your team. The gap is closed by creating a plan, putting it in motion, checking its progress, and acting to change direction, if needed, to meet your goals.

There's nothing new in this process; it's the management standard of the plan-do-check-act. We all know it by heart. This is where execution often fades into the sunset as just another initiative you didn't manage. It's easy to use the flavor-of-the-month management theme. When execution and results are the driving force behind your business, this situation changes.

How long will it take to close the gap? It's up to you. The change can come fast and hard, or it can move along at a snail's pace. You choose the pace of the business. I have a picture on my desk of a herd of horses running; its caption reads, "The Speed of the Leader Determines the Rate of the Pack." That's true. You set the pace. If you are urgent, if you are consistent, if you are focused, if you are clear in communicating your goals and expectations as a leader, your team will follow. It's up to you to lead the team. If they choose not to follow and keep up, they will get left behind in the dust created by the rest of the team.

CHAPTER 8
Vision, Mission, Values, and Goals

A critical part of the strategic planning process is having a clear vision, mission, values, and goals. If you are missing one of these important legs, it will be like eating Thanksgiving Day dinner at your dining room table with only three of the four legs on your chair. You will certainly end up on the floor at some point. Strategic plans are what closes your business's gap from the current state to the desired or expected state. Without these principles to guide your team, they can stray far off the path you have laid out. Consider these as guard-rails your business is going to use to stay on track during your trip down the business Autobahn.

You must consider the fact that all the processes in your business are intertwined. When you make a change in one area of your business, there will be consequential and perhaps unpredictable changes in other areas of your business. As MORE™ changes your business by closing the gaps, the strategies employed in one area of your business will impact the others.

At one point in my business, we decided if we imported a particular raw material we would benefit by a cost reduction of 20 percent. We began importing this material by the container load. (A typical container was around $30,000.) As we began importing, we realized we needed a safety stock much larger than we were accustomed to. This led to pressures on our cash flow. We also needed a place to put the two or three containers we needed to have to buffer possible interruptions in our material flow. This led to increased lease costs. You get the picture. The initial raw savings were not the total picture once we considered the impact on the entire business. MORE™ takes this into consideration. It views the business holistically and examines the ramifications of changes. The graphic below shows the overlapping of major areas of a business.

The MORE™ Business Dynamic Model

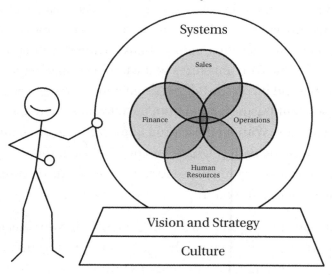

One more thing: you are responsible for implementing these four critical elements. Do not delegate these. It's important that you do this work. Collaborate with your team, but you have the final decision on the content. You own these.

Vision — What Your Business Will Become

What do you want to be when you grow up? That is not only
a question for children. It's a serious question for you and your business. What do you, the business owner and captain of the ship, want
your business to be? Do you see it? Where are you going?

Your vision statement is a forward-looking, aspirational statement about your business. This is the public declaration of your
business's highest-level goals. A written vision statement creates
a high-level focus of what the business will be like when it fulfills its
given purpose and direction.

It could sound like this for the Super Secure Safe Company:

> *We will be the largest regional producer of safes in the United
> States. We will deliver $40,000,000 in profitable sales by the
> end of 2015. We will offer the greatest total value and lead
> the market in technological innovation and product design.
> We will be the go-to value brand for our customers. We will
> give back to our community by helping families in need. We
> will have fun doing it.*

Make sure you are crystal clear about your vision statement. You
must own and live it. You must be able to succinctly and clearly
communicate it to your team and stakeholders. Practice saying
it. Is it real? Does it make sense with your goals and expectations
for the business?

It takes a great deal of time and carefully considered thought to
develop the vision for your business. Write it out, then have your
peers, friends, and loved ones review it with you and ask for their
constructive feedback. Take the time to get it right.

Mission — What Your Business Does

What is your purpose in life? Why are you here? Many of us struggle with this question throughout our lives. Many people have tried valiantly to answer this question.

For a business it's critical, even mandatory, to have a clear, concise, written mission statement. The mission statement explains the business's reason for existence, its purpose.

It could sound like this:

> *The mission of the Super Secure Safe Company is to create the highest quality safes for our customers, ones that like no other product, will allow them to be assured their valuables are safe and secure. All of our team members see this as their goal at Super Secure Safe and are committed to this mission with all the zeal and fervor they possess. We will make a profit for Super Secure Safe so it can sustain and support itself, its committed team members, and all stakeholders in the business.*

I know this sounds corny, but it's an example of why the company exists. Ask yourself why your business exists. Is it to provide you a comfortable living? To fill a customer's needs or wants? To provide a living for your team members? Make sure that you are clear about the purpose of the business. By the way, profit here is a given; you need to write it in. If you don't declare profit as a purpose, you can and will make products or provide services to fulfill your customer's needs to no end. The business will die without profits to sustain itself.

💬 *Why does your business exist?*

Your mission statement will guide the methods and decisions of your business. It answers the question about what you do.

If you do not clearly state the mission of your business, the same confusion will arise. Write it down, practice saying it, talk about it, and get feedback from your team, customers, and trusted advisors. Make it happen! You are responsible for this.

Values – How You Do What You Do

Who are you? Have you given much thought to this question? My conclusion is that we are the sum of our thoughts put into our actions — in other words: we are how we behave. You can choose to direct your actions in any number of ways, for good or for evil. What is your personal code of conduct? How do you treat others? How do you act in emotionally crucial times?

> *Who are you? How do you expect your business to behave?*

How do you expect your business to behave? How are your team members going to behave toward each other as they work on the business? How are you going to behave toward your customers? How are you going to treat your suppliers? How are you going to treat the other family members in and out of the business? How do you treat our community, city, state, and federal government? That last part caught you by surprise, didn't it? Yes, your business needs to have a code of conduct that governs all its internal and external relationships.

It could sound like this:

*We recognize that all of us are here for the same purpose
of making Super Secure Safe Company a successful and
respected business. We are servant leaders, and as such, we
have high standards for our behavior with everyone we come
into contact with as we perform our work inside and outside
of our business. We hold these behaviors as musts and will
call anyone out for not living these standards.*

*They include: we agree that other people matter more than
ourselves; we agree to show respect for everyone at all times;
we agree to disagree and not be disagreeable; we will be
truthful and always tell the truth, even when it is uncomfortable; and we will be graceful in our actions and speech.*

I recommend that you put the language of your value statement into
every job description and evaluation form you have and get every
team member to sign off on the values of the business. Review it with
everyone and call team members out when they cross the line.

This is a huge accountability item. Your expectation must be that
everyone at all times will adhere to the values of the company. This
extends above and beyond the "best interests of the company"
excuse. You, as the owner of the business, hold these values sacred.
If you overlook their importance or let your team get away with
transgressions of these values, you will be viewed as the stereotyp-
ical evil business owner. I am not exaggerating this point. I have
seen it in action. Live up to the values you hold dear, and that
drive your behavior.

Goals — The Current Finish Lines for Success

Are we there yet? If you have ever taken a vacation with small children and not-so-small adults, this question has probably come

up at least a million times. Why ask it? I am sure that you set out on vacation with a specific destination in mind. Did you tell your family, "Get in the car, and I will tell you when we get to where we are going?" That doesn't work, so don't try it. It will make the trip an agonizing journey.

Have you told your team where they are going? You can imagine the frustration level of your team not knowing where they are going. Clearly defined, clearly timed, and clearly communicated goals explain to your team where they are going and let them plan their actions to play their role in meeting the goal.

Technically speaking, a goal is an observable and measurable end result having one or more objectives within a fixed timeframe. This is classic business speak and a great answer. What does it look like or sound like?

How about this:

> *Super Secure Safe Company will increase its overall net profit by 13.75 percent during the fiscal year 2056. It will do this by maximizing the share of our existing customer base, and adding new customers that will contribute $1,000,000 in profit.*

We can measure this and observe it; it has objectives stated, and it has a timeframe for execution and result.

When reviewing the business's goals, they must be vetted for reasonableness. Setting a goal to increase profits and sales by 100 percent within a three-month period is not what anyone would call reasonable. In contrast, a goal that does not push your team or yourself does not grow the business. Goals are set by your vision for the business.

Goals are the roadmap by which success is measured. You will set intermediate goals within BIG goals. A BIG goal would be achieving an 18-percent sales increase year over year. There must be a plan behind the BIG goal that says how it will be achieved.

In most cases, the details of a plan that shows how you are going to reach a goal are what is missing. You and your team must be able to identify and write down the steps and actions that are necessary to reach a goal. Don't let your planning meetings become exercises in number generation. This was our planning process before we became a MORE™ company. We would look at the financials and generate numbers for sales, operations, delivery, and overhead; little thought was given to how we were going to reach those numbers and what actions needed to occur. We called it budgeting, but that was just another name for random number generation. After MORE™, we considered a larger set of influencers on our business. They included our competition's plans, labor-market pressures, the economy in general, key indicators for economic growth of our market space, and other soft issues that would impact our business and its profit generation.

> *We called it budgeting, but that was just another name for random number generation.*

Planning meetings should be idea-generating machines and include full discussions about how to reach the goals. You need to make them interactive and ensure everyone has input. Remember, this is not a plan for you, the owner; it's a plan for your team to reach the goals set by your vision of what the business can become.

Plans include detailed steps of how your team is going to reach the BIG goal. View the details of your plans as steps along the journey toward reaching that goal. It's your job to keep people and processes going down the path. In the plan-do-check-act cycle, it's your job to check, measure, and monitor progress for the agreed-upon goals.

I want to give you a couple of caveats. When you are setting long-term visionary goals for your business, they may lack specific details as to time of arrival and measurement. Don't let the rules of S.M.A.R.T. goals limit your thinking. (A S.M.A.R.T. goal is one that is specific, measurable, achievable, results-focused and time-bound.) Be bold and aggressive in setting the future direction of your business. The other point to consider here is that the long-term goals of your business may change due to circumstance or business environment. You need some flexibility as you plan the business's future direction and targets. We, as owners, tend to see the future of the business before our team. Our task is to be ahead of the team, planning what resources are needed, knowing when they must be available, and arranging for them to be ready when needed. This is working on the business, not in the business.

Goals have no meaning without measuring the progress your team is making. Everything can be measured. There are always numeric indicators of performance. I hate saying "always," because someone, somewhere will come up with an exception to the rule. So maybe it's better to say, "almost always." The point is that progress must be tracked to assess whether your business is acting urgently and focused toward reaching the goals.

💬 *Successfully planned goals are detailed, measurable, observable, and timed.*

Your team must regularly present to you the progress they are making toward their goals. If a plan is going sideways, your team is responsible for supplying to you the steps that are being taken to correct the issue, not the other way around. Celebrate with them the progress of making the plan reality. You may not realize it, but your approval and enthusiasm of excellent execution is as contagious as it is synergistic. Your team will draw energy from you; conversely, if all you tell them is it's not good enough, you will discourage them into submission. Be excited and get your team excited about their direction, too. Measure progress toward the goals regularly.

Crossing the Goal

CHAPTER 9

Review the Interviews, SWOT Analysis, and Gap Analysis with Ownership

Be Brave; Reality Bites

The next step in our journey is to review the interviews, SWOT analysis, and gap analysis — all the information gathered up to this point — with your MORE™ advisor. This is a candid view of how your business really is, not how you think it is. These two views can and will be very different.

When I went through this review, I believed that the team was aligned with the goals and direction of the business. Reality could not have been further from the truth. It was embarrassing and discomforting to know that my perception was not the team's reality. I believed I was a better manager than that. I felt I was communicating in a direct and respectful manner with the team. I was wrong, and that hurt. It takes courage to admit that you are part of the problem with your business. It was the discomfort I had been feeling about the business, but I didn't know how to identify the causes of that discomfort. MORE™ brought everything to the surface so we could address the issues and remove the roadblocks to success.

💬 *It was embarrassing and discomforting, but worth it.*

Sharing Results with Key Team Members

After the findings have been shared with you, the owner, schedule a follow-up meeting with key team members. These team members consist of the group that is responsible for the running of the business. They currently are expected to perform the processes of the company. You may also wish to include team members for whom the information being communicated will impact how they perform their role in the team.

During this meeting, the findings of the interviews, SWOT and gap analysis, and financials are reviewed. Also shared during this meeting are goals and projects of high priority that have been revealed as necessary to the business. This is not a complete listing of what's needed to move the business toward your goals; other items will be added to this list as work on the business continues.

It's Not You; It's Me

This section of MORE™ reminds me of the *Seinfeld* skit where George's girlfriend takes a non-confrontational approach to ending their relationship by saying, "It's not you. It's me." In reality, it's everyone on the team including you. Your team may try to put the responsibility on themselves. They don't want to hurt your feelings or put their jobs in jeopardy by stating the truth about you and your business. Be brave and take it like an owner and leader. A little *mea culpa* goes a long way with your team. All truly great leaders are willing to own up to their behavior and make changes. Be the leader of your team and don't play the blame game. Recognize the problem, own it, and do something about it. This is what leaders do.

💬 *Be brave. This is what leaders do.*

Deciding What to Share and with Whom

You must be judicious about what information you share and who needs what information at what level of the business. The rule of thumb is to gauge what information is needed by a team member or group of individuals so that they can understand their role in helping the business making a profit. It's important to get as much information as low in the organization as possible so the team can make quick and accurate decisions.

💬 *They didn't understand the role they played in the business making money.*

The team can be overwhelmed by information they don't understand. If your business's leaders don't understand how to read financials and interpret them, you need to educate them. This must be detailed and will take several repetitions and some one-on-one tutoring. It's an investment in time with a quick payback for the business. Most of our team leaders had been with the business for more than 10 years and didn't understand the information presented on the financials. Granted, they understood the bottom line, but they had no clue about what happened between the top line and the bottom line. They didn't understand the role they played in the business making money. Considerable time and effort was spent in explaining how their roles contributed to our success. It was worth the time and effort and paid off handsomely for the business.

Transparency About the Condition and Direction for the Business

Let's discuss the role of transparency. If you believe that your team cannot see right through you, you are wrong. They have been around you enough to tell when something doesn't make sense or seem right. Be open, honest, and direct in your statements. Shading the truth or lying is not an attractive character trait for a leader. In fact, the entire re-engineering will come to a grinding halt if the team feels they are being led in a direction under false pretenses.

When your team can clearly see your goals, where you want to take the business, their role, and your expectations of them in the business, they can put context around what goals they need to set and what criteria they will use to make decisions. Conversely, if you're unclear and communicate the goals in a confusing manner, they won't have any reference for making decisions.

Consider your GPS and how it works. You input your destination: the street address, city, state, and ZIP code. It then calculates a route based on the parameters you set up: tolls, no tolls, highways, avoid construction, etc., etc. The GPS is clear about where you want to go and how you want to get there. The same concept applies to your team. You must clearly and directly tell them the destination, your vision, and your goals. Once that is done, you must plainly communicate with them how you want to accomplish the goals, your mission, and your values. Be clear and direct when you communicate. Check and see if your team can repeat what you have said back to you if they understand the meaning behind your words, and how they would behave based on the instructions you've just given them.

Make sure everyone on the team understands your communication. It's vital for them to be able to translate these core representations of the business into strategic goals for their part of the business. Take the time to sit down with them one-on-one and ask them about the vision, mission, values, and goals. If they can talk with you about it in a conversational manner, congratulations; you may have successfully communicated. Now it's time to observe their behavior and see if they put the words into action. If you observe behavior in a team member that is not congruent, then work with them and tell them the importance of what they are doing as it relates to the success of the business.

What Are You Going to Do?

💬 *It made things happen.*

The decision to share this information can be very uncomfortable for you personally as the business's owner. I know it was for me. But it is what it is. The question a leader asks is, "What am I going to do about it?" To make this decision, the information review must be accompanied by a big measure of courage. It took me a while to get comfortable with the position of relating that our business was not being what it could be, that it needed to change and the sooner, the better. Not everyone on the leadership team agreed with this, and that added to my discomfort in moving forward. The one determining factor for me was that it was the right thing to do. Regardless of the obstacles in front of us, we needed to change our thinking. I have no regrets about the decision to share our information. It made things happen.

CHAPTER 10
Kickoff Meeting with Key Team Members

The next step in the process is to have a meeting with all your key team members. The purpose is to begin to get everyone on the same page and ask for their commitment in moving the business forward. Make sure you clearly communicate why you are re-engineering your business.

During this meeting, you will set the tone of urgency and enthusiasm for the journey with your team. The more you project your willingness to change the way you are thinking about your business the more people will understand that they must adopt the same mindset.

> *You set the tone of urgency and enthusiasm.*

Do not overlook the importance and impact of this meeting on your team members. This meeting is designed to produce real, cohesive communication for the team from the information gathered during the owner interview, the DISC personality assessment test, the key team member interviews, and the SWOT, gap, and financial analysis. The purpose of this meeting is to present information to the team to get them on the same page while producing strategic plans to close the gaps.

The gaps that are discussed in the meeting are the result of the analysis of where you are operationally in all areas as compared to where you should be to create the maximum value in the business. One example of this is found in the sales plan. Before MORE™, we built our yearly budget based on a forecast using only product line and customer sales. With MORE™, we built a budget and sales plan using goals by individual customer and the specific tactics by customer that we would apply to reach the sales goal. We budgeted our sales by account, product line, and sometimes down to the individual product level, depending on the customer type. This was an identified gap in our kickoff meeting. The work put into closing this gap was extraordinary. We developed automated reports to track the weekly sales activities associated with each account. We closed the gap from where we were to where we needed to be to create value in the business.

How much information you have shared with the team in the past will determine the intensity of their reaction to what they are being shown. My team was in the dark. They had no idea about the financial condition of the business or how we made profit — only that we, the owners, would be in a good mood or a bad mood, which they assumed resulted from good or bad news about the business. They didn't know how to read the financials we presented, so we took the time to educate them about the financials and how the business made money.

💬 *My team was in the dark.*

We showed the team the high-level financial results from the past 20 years. Talk about baring your soul in public. It was intimidating. The team had no idea, zero, zip, none about where we had been and where we were financially or strategically.

The first time the team was exposed to the financials, they were amazed. They had no idea of the scale and scope of our operation. They didn't understand how narrow our profit margins were at times. It was a total "deer in the headlights" moment for the entire team. Some of the team members had been with us for more than 20 years and had no idea how important a role they played in our business. It not only opened their eyes, but it opened their minds to think differently about what they were doing each day. This was a painful lesson for me to learn. What if we had shared our financials 10 years earlier? We would have been well down the road on our journey to increased revenue and profit. Instead, we were afraid that if they "knew the truth" our team members would react negatively. It was quite the opposite, the revealing of our financials invigorated them to make our goals.

> *It not only opened their eyes, but it opened their minds to think differently about what they were doing each day.*

Transparency in the Kickoff Meeting

It's important to be transparent and open in the kickoff meeting. If the team feels you are anything but straightforward with the information about the business, they will not communicate openly with you. The clearer you are about the true state of the business, not your perception of the business, the greater the depth of conversation that will be generated about the business and how it must change to produce value. Done well, it's like the result of the collision that happens in a particle; the energy created opens the business for inspection in its most intimate and basic parts. It's a deconstruction of the business, allowing reverse engineering to deliver increased value.

Transparency is a key characteristic of great leaders. When you are transparent about the condition of the business, you put yourself and the business out for everyone to see. Transparency builds trust; without trust, you will not be followed. You know what they call a leader with no one following? Alone. You cannot take this journey alone; it's not possible to address all the issues quickly and efficiently alone. You need your team to trust you, and you need to lead them.

Courage

This meeting with all your key team members takes courage. So, buck it up, buckaroo, and suck it up, buttercup. Take responsibility for the faults, foibles, and lack of profitability in your business. It hurts. Trust me; I have bought the t-shirt that says, "I have failed you, my team." It takes real courage to be open and admit your mistakes as the leader of your business. It's also encouraging and inspiring to your team. They see that you are willing to accept reality, change, grow, and become a better leader for them and the business.

Your team will not come out and say it to your face, but they will have hoped and waited for this change in you and your business. They know how great the business can become when you step up your game as a leader and move them forward. You will see it in your team's expressions and actions as you move the business forward and change yourself. They are waiting on you, their leader, to make the first move, so summon all your resolve and courage and get out there and get moving!

Changing your thinking is difficult. You must change your thinking, or you will become the roadblock in your business to success. You as the leader of the business must redirect the thinking of your team. That can be more challenging and takes more effort on your part. At the same time, as you are changing, you are helping them navigate the same changes in their thinking.

The entire MORE™ process of re-engineering the business is explained to your team, what your goals for the business are, the first steps that will be taken, the deliverables from those initial steps, and that there will be a follow-up meeting for the team to report the findings from the interviews, SWOT analysis, and gap analysis, and there will be strategic plans made, implemented and executed.

The kickoff meeting is a time for them to ask questions. The more questions the better. It allows your team to voice their concerns and get information as to what will be required of them. During one kickoff meeting the question was raised, "Why will these guys be any different from the three previous groups in here? They are all the same. All they did was give us changes to make and then leave." After working in that business for 60 days, a team member offered the following compliment: "This really is different. It's all about the success of both the business and us (the people in the business)." This spells out exactly why MORE™ is totally different.

MORE™ is all about working with you, the owner and your team to achieve your goals. This is a side-by-side walk down the path to meet your goals. It involves a passionate determination to achieve your aims as the owner of the business. MORE™ demands you and your team work in and on your business hands-on and with your feet on the ground.

Personality Assessment Team Results

As described earlier, the personality assessment results portray how the team will likely interact with each other and make decisions. The individual results have been shared with the individual team members during the interview process. It shows how they will possibly act as a team in consideration of each person's strengths and weaknesses. This information allows them to be aware of how they should possibly act and interact with other members of the team.

CHAPTER 11
Core MORE™ Concepts
the Business Must Embrace

We are making a side trip here to look at some core concepts your business must embrace to be successful: communication, transparency, demolishing silos, expectations, accountability, and urgency. These ideas have been laced throughout the book. We need to discuss them and make sure their meaning is clear to you and your team. Some of the terms are bantered about as business jargon; however, saying a word and manifesting the behavior of a term are two different things. These are terms that describe how your business must behave to be successful. MORE™ is dependent on these characteristics of how your team behaves with each other and with key stakeholders.

Communication

No single word has been analyzed more than communication. Communication is the key to forming and maintaining all relationships. A business is dependent on the relationships it maintains. Therefore, clear, direct communication is essential for your business to be successful. I made communication in my business my responsibility. I wanted to make sure anyone and everyone affected by the actions we took in our business understood what was going on and why.

Think about the many relationships your business maintains: customers, owners, managers, suppliers, and team members, just to name a few. What happens if you decide not to communicate with your customers? What happens if you decide it's better for two people on your team not to communicate? All scenarios that result in a breakdown of communication are laden with disaster for your business. In your role as the top leader of your business, this is a crucial matter.

Getting the right information to the right people is a daunting task. It requires a view of the business process and organization that few people besides you possess. Information that is important to some of your team members means nothing to others. This can be a problem in meetings: TMI, Too Much Information. Be judicious about the complete sharing of information. It can make meetings a slogging ritual. Vomiting information out for information's sake is not communication; it's vomit, one big mess. Communicate what is important for the entire group to hear, then communicate information more specific to your team members' roles in different settings. It's a judgment and requires knowledge of your organization and business process.

⟲ *Get the right information to the right people.*

I also have learned that it's not necessarily what you say but how you say it that counts. I have faced this dilemma many times. If I was irritated, my words would come out sounding harsh and pointed. The person to whom the statement was directed would assume my ire was directed at them when that was not the case. Make sure you hear yourself when you communicate.

Communication must be direct and open to be effective. I've always considered how the person I was communicating with would hear my words. Their experiences and filters are not like yours. Think about their personality profile and adjust your speech to fit how they will hear the words.

Timeliness of communication has a direct impact on the execution of plans. I bet you have never heard this phrase in your business: "When did you know this?" Someone was left out of the loop. More often than not, since they didn't know the information, their job performance could be under the gun. Again, I cannot overemphasis that communication in your business takes a great deal of knowledge about your business and its processes. When you don't thoroughly communicate, product introductions can be delayed, personnel actions delayed, and detrimental results can occur.

Communication is not only a practical matter of execution but also of respect for the person with whom you are communicating. We were always honest and open with our written and spoken communication. We were honest to a fault, even though sometimes being honest was not the greatest feeling. It hurt people's feelings, but in the long run, everyone knew where they stood, regardless of whether the information being transmitted was good or bad. Your team and the stakeholders of your business may not like what is said; however, in the end, they will appreciate the respect you showed them by being clear and direct with your words.

💬 *Communication is not only a practical matter of execution but also of respect.*

A MORE™ business makes sure that information is communicated throughout the organization in a timely fashion to team members and stakeholders who need it to operate the business successfully.

Transparency

We discussed transparency in the previous chapter. Transparency, in a nutshell, is both sharing and not hiding information about your business.

Hidden agendas are a form of not being transparent. Transparency is at the other end of the spectrum. Be open with your plans for the business. Be direct with team members about violations of the values that you want your business to embody. Do not tolerate your team or anyone who works with your business to be disrespected.

Transparency becomes hard and uncomfortable when you share financial information with your team. We are all excited about our results when we have a record-setting month, year, or day. What does it feel like to share a month that's a train wreck? Both good and bad results are information. The good results prompt you to ask what you did so you can repeat the results. The bad results prompt you to ask what you did so you can avoid repeating the results. Financial results are the measuring tape of the success of your business. If your team doesn't know how they are doing against your goals — or for that matter don't know your goals — how can they work in their role to make the business successful?

💬 *Transparency starts with you.*

A MORE™ business needs transparency to deliver the expected goals of the business owner. It starts with you and filters down to your team. Do not become the emperor in your new clothes.

Demolishing Silos

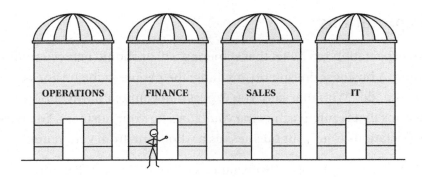

As I discussed earlier, organizational silos make for ineffective, inefficient, micromanaged, stagnant businesses that have about zero probability of growth. A traditional silo situation — and it was huge in our business — exists between sales and manufacturing operations, that seem to have opposite goals. Sales wants to please the customer with anything they can dream up or desire. Manufacturing wants to have just three products so they can be efficient. These silos aren't effective for the business. They don't talk to each other. They aren't working on the success of the business; they only want to produce success for their silo. If they don't communicate about the problems each is experiencing, there won't be success for the business. Can't we all get along and produce successful results for the business?

> 💬 *Silos make ineffective, inefficient, micro-managed, stagnant businesses.*

A MORE™ business has no tolerance for silos. It has no boundaries between teams, departments, or divisions. They are moving fast toward their goals and cannot stand the static that is created with silos. They are one team with one goal: one for all and all for one. The team and its leaders operate in the best interest of the business as a whole at all times. Success is achieved together, or it's not success.

Expectations

An expectation is a belief that someone will or should achieve something. A business doesn't do anything; the people in the business are the "do." With that said, you expect that your team will perform actions that result in achieving your goals for your business. You have expectations from your business as a whole and from your team.

There are many levels of expectations in your business. If you're a manufacturer, there are expectations of each manufacturing operation, each operator, each manager, each salesperson, each scheduler, each computer, each piece of technology, each material, and each finished product. Expectations should abound in your business. These are communicated as goals, standards of production, sales goals, on-boarding procedures, or any other metric that you expect someone to achieve.

The problem with expectations in our business was that we never bothered to write down our expectations; we just expected everyone to intuitively know what was expected. It sounds crazy, doesn't it? It was. It was a guessing game played by everyone on the team. When we became a MORE™ business, we wrote our expectations down.

💬 *We never bothered to write down our expectations.*

We communicated these expectations with a document we called "Job Responsibilities and Expectations." Everyone had one of these documents. Each team member and their immediate leader reviewed, approved, and signed it and was held accountable for the expectations in the document. The document clearly explained what each team member would be expected to achieve. It documented the role the team member played in the success of the business.

A MORE™ business clearly and in great detail, communicates what is expected of the business and each team member, including the top leader.

Accountability

The Merriam-Webster online dictionary defines accountability as "the quality or state of being accountable; especially: an obligation or willingness to accept responsibility or to account for one's actions."

Accountability is all about responsibility. When I signed my Job Responsibility and Expectations document as CEO, I accepted the responsibility to guide the business to meet the goals of the business as defined by the stockholders. I made plans, delegated actions to others, and took actions to move the business to fulfill the goals of the stockholders. When all was said and done, I was responsible for the results of the business. You are responsible for the results of your business.

> ⟲ *Accountability is all about responsibility.*

You have greater accountability as the business owner. You are accountable to everyone in the business for the results of the business. Your responsibility doesn't end there; your team members have families. We had well over 70 families that depended on our business for their livelihood. I took it very personally. They were my responsibility; they were my team. I was accountable to them for producing results that would grow the business and provide opportunity for them to grow personally and professionally.

A MORE™ business holds everyone responsible for their actions. It doesn't accept excuses. There are reasons, however. Work on the reasons and turn them into successes. Accountability begins at the top and goes all the way down the organization to its foundation. You are accountable for the culture of accountability in your business. It begins with you.

Urgency

Urgency implies a call for immediate attention and action. Do it now! Let's do something now! I didn't need a dictionary for this definition. I know it well, and I was the chief offender of not acting quickly with purpose in our business until I realized what it cost us.

GOAL

Running fast now!

Urgency is a missing piece of most business cultures. Businesses take the attitude that it will all work out. It may, but it may not. Either way, things will definitely take longer. The sooner you change your business, the longer you have to enjoy the benefits of the new, re-engineered, and more profitable business.

"Why should we be in a hurry to change?" "We are comfortable with the way things are going." "If we need to change we can do it later." "Just give it time, and it will work out on its own." I remember thinking and saying every one of these statements. Have you? It's very easy to ignore crucial business issues and let them work out on their own. What is it costing to not address them now?

In his book *A Sense of Urgency*, John P. Kotter states that, based on his research, 76 percent of all strategic plans are never implemented. Think about the energy, focus, time, and money put into developing those plans, all wasted. Did someone in those businesses not see the need to immediately implement those plans? If they did see the need, why didn't they follow through?

Resources are precious and must be allocated on a priority basis for the majority of small businesses. Using those limited resources in developing the strategic plans that will move the business forward and not executing them is a terrible waste of the business's resources. Priority and focus must be applied to the goals that are important. Quickly execute the plan. This is the responsible way for you and your team to manage and measure the movement to your strategic goals.

💬 *Quickly execute the plan.*

A MORE™ business is all about moving and acting to reach its goals with urgency. It's proactive in addressing its issues and making strategic plans to reach its goals. It moves quickly toward the goals, realizing that the faster it achieves the goals, the more time the business will benefit from the gain.

Measurement

MORE™ is about measuring improvement. This is the important part of taking the journey. What key metrics are important to gauge if you are making progress in your plans. Where are you now? Where do you want to be? How far have you come on your journey? What do you need to do to get where you are going? You must have a written, communicated plan, or it's like taking a drive and not caring where you end up. You must have a very specific idea where you want to go, so you must measure and plan.

CHAPTER 12
Development of Strategic Plans

A strategy is a plan of action or a policy that is developed to achieve a goal or a value of your business. A strategic plan is a document stating what your team is going to do, how it's going to do it, and how it will know when it has been achieved. It's a result of purposeful, intentional managers and their teams. In your business, the strategic plan will provide clarity, guardrails, and standards for making decisions and allocating resources.

A successfully formed strategic plan must be populated with several requisite items. They are: a clearly defined goal, an owner, a timeline, a definition of what success is, defined metrics by which progress and the success of the plan will be measured, and a detailed step-by-step process of how your business will reach the goal.

Successful plans are a result of collaboration across the functional areas of your business. If the business has silo issues, it won't have the robust discussions and necessary input to generate strategic plans that will move it ahead. There must be involvement across all areas of your business to understand the issues each will encounter due to the changes in their areas developed by the plan itself.

One-Year Plan
Fiscal Year 20XX Strategic Plan

Our Vision _____

Our Mission _____

Core Values _____

THE GOAL
Critical Success Factors

Objective:	Objective:
Measurement:	Measurement:
Tactics:	Tactics:

Signature below indicates agreement to the strategic plan outlined above.

Approved by _____ Date _____

Approved by _____ Date _____

Approved by _____ Date _____

Once the goal has been achieved, it's time to celebrate. With many goals, once your team has achieved the goal, there is another element for continuing success. The process or policy that you put in place must be owned by someone and managed. A team owning the process or policy is not as effective as an individual owning it. Beyond that, strategic plans must also be vigorously reviewed continuously to see if they still meet the needs of the business in the changing environment. If they don't or if they could be more effective, a new plan must be laid out to improve the results. It's a continuous cycle of improving your business. Far too many plans die after being implemented and never evolve to the point of providing maximum benefit to the business.

Strategic planning takes place on several levels. There are plans that dictate processes in the day-to-day operations of the business to meet its goals. There are plans that focus on a specific issue and how to improve performance. There are plans that assess the team members that are needed to take the business to the next level. Plans should be made for the successful transfer or transition of the business itself to the next team of leaders. Your job as chief leader of your business is to manage the business's set of plans, not to manage the implementation of the plans. Work on the business, not in the business. Create the value in the business, not in yourself.

Timelines and the timing of plans are an area to address. Most businesses have plans for the current year of operation. It's essential for you as an owner to look beyond this year's horizon and plot the course for years to come. Some traditional timeframes for businesses are three-, five-, and ten-year plans. More businesses are adopting rolling budgets, which would necessitate rolling strategic plans with each new budget. Have you considered a generational plan?

There are also instances of scenario planning. Scenario planning takes into account disruptive changes to your business. The changes considered can involve the leadership, revenue, suppliers, the business climate, the competition, or any other factor that could grossly alter your business's course. What happens if you die or become disabled or mentally impaired? That would certainly be disruptive to your business.

⊘ Strategic plans for all functional areas of business.

A MORE™ business contains strategic plans for all functional areas. It is continually involved in measuring the success of its plans. It continuously improves its plans to meet goals. It collaborates across all functional areas. It makes plans that consider the disruptive forces that could come to bear on the business through what-if scenarios. It knows where it's going and how it's going to get there.

⊘ MORE™ was an investment, not a cost to our business.

In my business, we addressed our purchasing process immediately. Before MORE™, we had good relations with our vendors and had negotiated with them successfully over the years. Our raw-material cost was well above 40 percent of selling cost. Purchasing well was a necessity for our success. With MORE™ we developed a strategic plan for our purchasing. We developed a process of negotiation that addressed our needs for lower costs. We spent time considering all the elements of purchasing vendor by vendor and planned how we would lower our materials costs by vendor. We also considered our product merchandising and identified cost reductions that would help us in product innovation, development, and introduction. The result was more than astonishing. Hold on; here is the result: We lowered our material costs by over $1,000,000 across the next year. Yes, that is a one followed by six zeros. MORE™ was an investment, not a cost to our business.

Decisions, Decisions, Decisions

At the core of making strategic plans is the process by which you make decisions. You probably fall into several categories when making decisions. At either extreme of the decision pendulum swing are pits that will trap you.

One extreme encompasses the desire to fix the issue now. There isn't adequate consideration of the opportunity or challenge. Assumptions are made as to the root cause of the issue. (You know what assuming does, right? It never fails.) Without carefully ascertaining the root cause of the problem, you will fix the wrong thing, which is always a disaster. Also on this side of the pendulum swing is acting too quickly without consideration of how the issue plays into the overall scheme of change. Changing out of sequence and without planning will create a domino effect and will lead to greater issues for the team.

At the other extreme, you delay making decisions because you need more information. You want to be 100 percent, totally convinced that what you decide is going to be correct. Even at the best of times, all the data in the world is only going to give you a best choice, not a solid "yes." The amount of information a decision requires must be tempered with the urgency to make the decision. Decision-making is as much an art as a science. The more you make decisions, the more you become comfortable with not having full information. And there is no such thing as full information, as I alluded to before.

In our business, we liked delaying decisions. We always thought the issues would work themselves out given enough time, and we would not need to have the difficult conversations. This tendency stunted our progress toward our goal. Key team members were not producing to their full capabilities and therefore were impeding progress. They couldn't see or suggest a better way to get the job done and create value for the business. We recognized the problems with these team members but never did anything about them. These were difficult conversations we needed to have about expected performance. Even when we had the difficult conversations, we didn't act when our expectations weren't met. Everyone received the benefit of the doubt as they presented excuses and we gave them another chance. Sometimes the excuses were addressed, and we still gave them another chance when the expectations or goals were not met. This resulted in a huge morale problem. Team members who were diligently pursuing and achieving success saw what went on with the non-performers and questioned why they worked hard to add value to the business. We changed our practices, but it was hard to break the cycle we had established.

I taught Tae Kwon Do for fifteen years and achieved the rank of Fourth Degree Black Belt. We would practice the same moves over and over and over in Tae Kwon Do class. It conditioned us to act, not react to circumstances. The moves were all actions to an action by your opponent. When we taught self-defense, we asked the students to imagine a dark alley where they had their backs up against a fence with several unsavory characters wanting to make hamburger meat out of their face and providing them no conceivable escape. The purpose of the exercise was to make them think about how they would address the problem. What would they do? What choices would they make: run, stand and fight, take the beating, or — my favorite — act like a crazy person. Good research shows that the more you envision a scenario and the possible actions that can be taken, the more likely you are to make a decision, accept your action, and survive the situation.

⚬ *You can be a Black Belt in decision-making by practicing.*

You can be a Black Belt in decision-making by practicing your decision-making over and over. Think about what-if scenarios, the worst possible case, the best case, and the actions that you would take under certain circumstances. What would be your trigger points? What would be the actions you can see yourself taking? How would you enlist and deploy your team and its talents to meet the scenario? How are you, your team, and the business going to survive the situation? Envision and think about the circumstances that would lead you to make the decision. The worst option is to not decide and not act, to just be carried by the circumstances, instead of thinking and planning out the actions. Will you react or act? There is a big difference in outcomes for your business and your team. This is working on your business, not in your business.

Emotions play a large role in the way you make decisions. We business owners are not the cool and calculating individuals we want to think we are or that are portrayed in the media. I laid awake at night, worrying about the impact of the decisions we were making, especially when the decisions impacted people's lives. Some of the most emotional decisions I had to make concerned the sale of our business. I agonized and cried about making the decision to sell the business. It was highly emotional. It impacted everyone in our family and in our business — well over 100 people in all. Each of those families had an average of three people, so the number of people became mind-boggling. I had relationships of some type with almost everyone in our business. I knew their families. It had a deep emotional impact on me on the day the sale became final. I intellectually knew it was the right decision to make. Yet when my emotions played on me, I worried about everyone. When you make decisions, your emotions will be an influence, so be prepared.

Bias plays a hidden role in decision-making most times. This is about how you perceive how the world and your business work and how you perceive the culture and the morale of your business. Bias often comes out in statements like "We have always done it this way." Yes, you are biased. You like the way you and your business do things. It's comfortable. You use the same criteria and metrics to define the path to your decision. They worked before; why not now? The challenge is to change the way you think about your business and move your bias in a new direction. The velocity and environment of your business are speeding up and changing on an hourly basis. Your decision-making process must adapt to an ever-changing business environment. The tried and true standards by which you made decisions in the past will probably not apply.

Have you considered the assumptions that your team makes in the decision processes of your business? You don't know what you don't know. This has always been a worrisome statement for me. Base your decisions on sound processes and assumptions about the businesses. Plan your decision-making just as you make strategic plans for all areas of your business.

What causes strategic plans to fail? At the top of my list is no planning. As the saying goes, "Failing to plan is planning to fail." If you don't know where you are going, you will never get there.

💬 *A MORE™ business uses clearly articulated goals and strategic plans that drive the business.*

Having a comprehensive and actionable planned strategy allows you to create engagement, alignment, and ownership within your business. It's a clear roadmap that shows where you've been, where you are, and where you're going next.

Other causes of strategic plan failure are:

- Failure to understand your market and customers
- Opening a business in an industry that isn't profitable
- Failure to understand and communicate what you are selling
- Inadequate financing
- Reactive attitudes
- Over-dependence on a single customer
- No customer strategy
- Not knowing when to say no
- Poor management
- Poor leadership
- Failure to own a plan
- Not setting deadlines or timelines for the plan
- Not having a plan

A MORE™ business uses clearly articulated goals and strategic plans that drive the business. It also has known values and a mission that guides decisions made on a day-to-day basis and in formulating strategic plans for the growth and transition of the business.

CHAPTER 13
Succession and Transition Plans

I want to make a disclaimer before I start talking about succession and transition plans. I'm not an expert and don't pretend to have enough knowledge of your business's situation, the legal aspects, or tax consequences to recommend exit strategies or discuss the tax implications or legal ramifications for you, your family, or your business. I am only able to share my experiences and knowledge as they relate to the transition in our business. I will tell you there is no substitute for outstanding legal and tax counsel. Seek out the best you can find and work with them. They will make you money. They did for me and my family during our transaction.

When are you going to leave your business? This is a frightening question for most of us. Your business is an important part of your identity and defines your purpose. It's very difficult to separate yourself from your business emotionally and physically. It's your baby, your creation. It has supported you for your career and provided for your family. It's hard to imagine life without your business, isn't it? It was very difficult for me. I would tear up at the thought of not being able to go to the factory and work. It was in large part how I defined and saw myself. But I did get over it.

The one thing that is certain in your life is that you will die. If you die while you are still chief leader, your business will undergo a transition. It will have a traumatic change in its chief leadership and ownership if you do not plan for the change. Is this the legacy you want to leave your family and team? The responsible thing to do is make plans and be sure they are communicated to your family and your team.

⌕ *When are you going to leave your business?*

Here is a partial list of questions that need to be considered:

- What do I need to have from this business to live the life to which my family and I have grown accustomed?
- What do I want for my entire team in my business?
- What does my family want from the business on a go-forward basis?
- Are there family members who should be considered for succession?
- How will a family member pay out the owners for the business?
- How will I be supported in the manner to which I am accustomed when I cut back or retire from the business?
- Is a non-family successor for my business the best answer, even if there are family members involved in the business?
- Should we look at an Employee Stock Ownership Plan?
- What if a strategic buyer makes us an offer?
- What if venture capital wants to buy us and roll us into their portfolio?
- Do I want to work for someone else?

- What would the terms of my/our employment be with new owners?

- If I sell, will I get all cash or will I have to carry some of the financing myself?

In the history of our business, we were approached in earnest three times to sell our business. The forms included strategic buyers, venture capital doing a roll-up of the same type of businesses, and strategic buyers rolling up manufacturers. Some of the attempts didn't offer us or our family adequate financial terms.

The crux of the matter is to determine the terms in which you want to exit your business. How do you see that happening? When do you see that happening? Do you know what are acceptable terms to you to exit? Do you have plans for multiple opportunities if they arise?

> *The crux of the matter is to determine the terms upon which you want to exit your business.*

Much focus is placed on the financial, legal, and tax planning process of business transition. There is much more for you to consider. The business itself must be prepared culturally and organization-ally. It must be goal driven to derive maximum value for you and your family. If you do not prepare, you are leaving the table with money still on it.

We started the process of preparing our business for transition when we changed our business with MORE™. It took us five years to change our business to an entity where it was the value and we, the owners, were not the value. While you are running your business, you will be simultaneously planning how you will exit it and what will happen to it after you leave. This is your responsibility to yourself, your family, and the families that rely on your business for their livelihood.

⊘ *Start planning now!*

I know of business owners who in their late 70s have said they needed to start planning what was going to happen to their businesses after they left. In all but a few rare exceptions that's too late. Your runway for developing and growing your business is short; without intense outside help and change, it's a daunting task. Start planning now!

We began with a series of meetings during which we outlined and set parameters of what each of the stockholders expected to gain from an exit from the business, regardless of the model of the transition. We also worked on what the business needed to provide to the family in a transition. These agreed-upon metrics were the basis of our guidelines for vetting any offer, succession plan, or transition.

Our personal metrics addressed our personal takeaway from the business, how the family debt to the business would be handled, under what circumstances we would stay and work for the new ownership, and how the factory real estate would be handled.

We also addressed some legacy questions. What would happen to our team? What would it mean to the licensing group that we belonged to? Would the business continue as an entity providing for our teams?

We discussed the characteristics of the optimal purchaser of our business. Venture, leveraged family member, outside manager, and strategic buyer types were all considered. We considered the overall characteristics of each type of transaction. We put a great deal of time and thought into a plan for succession or transition.

I thought of transition as the ultimate sale that our business would make. There was no more important sale or change. This change in the business would impact every stakeholder. With that thought in mind, gauge what time and energy you would put into the planning before you reach that point. The planning will make you money.

MORE™ addresses the cultural, organizational, and goal-driven changes to make the business, not you, the value of the business. If you are the value of the business, what happens when you leave the business? If you attract funds from outside, you will be working for the new owners. Is that acceptable to you? I don't know about you, but after 38 years of working for myself, I didn't find that attractive at all.

> ❍   *If you are the value of the business, what happens when you leave the business?*

CHAPTER 14
What Happened?

The End Result of MORE™

The conclusion is that we sold our business to a buyer within our industry. We achieved the financial metrics we had agreed upon. The family debt was eliminated, and we received a lease on our factory real estate.

The business is continuing and providing livelihoods for our team. The purchasers brought with them the sales acumen and sophistication to add substantial revenue, to provide security for our team. They also brought the ability to upgrade and automate the factory to become a more efficient producer.

I don't want to mislead you; the purchaser is not us, and they do things differently than we did. That is change, and change is hard, no matter the circumstances.

An additional family legacy issue was accomplished that was connected to the transaction. It had always been the dream of my father to grow the licensing structure to which we belonged into a true national brand. Our purchasers had the experience and capital investment that would allow them to become a true force in the competitive marketplace. His dream came true because of this transaction.

The transaction afforded the family stockholders the opportunity to pursue other opportunities. We are following our dreams and doing what we want to do to make a difference in other people's lives. My brothers stayed on for three months after the transaction to help with the transition. I left the business the day of the transaction. (They agreed, I had the better end of the deal. It's hard working for someone else when you are accustomed to making decisions on your own.)

I love business and in particular, family businesses just like yours. Personally, I have been able to follow my passions. In becoming an advisor with my mentor, I have committed myself to helping businesses and their teams to become successful. Nothing is more important than the success and growth of your business. Lewis and I take your success personally.

MORE™ allowed us to create value in our business by changing our thinking about our business. We made the business the value someone was looking for, independent of the value we added to the business.

Consider the philanthropy factor of your business. Each year that we didn't change and drive our value up, we lost the gain no matter the transition scenario. For example, imagine you can find just $50,000 that drops to your bottom line annually. The cost of not changing your business for ten years is that you gave away $500,000 to another person or business. Do not unwittingly be a philanthropist.

When are you going to start using MORE™? Why are you holding you back? The delay is keeping you from reaping the gains that come from thinking differently about your business and using MORE™ to get you more.

💬 *Does this make sense? What are you going to do?*

ABOUT THE AUTHORS

Lee Quinn

lee@rudyandassociates.com

Lee Quinn works with business owners who want to change their trajectory and momentum. Lee crafts, with the owners, plans to move the business forward and participates with them to execute their plans. Lee's goals are to make the business and its team successful and sustainable for the owner.

After a successful 38-year career of managing his family's consumer goods manufacturing business and holding numerous positions in the business, Lee served as CEO from 2006-2016, exiting with the business's sale.

Lee graduated from Eastern Kentucky University with a Bachelor's in Marketing. At the time of this book's publication, Lee was enrolled in the Entrepreneurship MBA program at the University of Louisville.

Lewis Rudy

lewis@rudyandassociates.com

Lewis Rudy is Founder and President of Rudy and Associates. Lewis works with business owners and their teams to build strong, intentional business growth. He identifies, isolates and eliminates the root causes of margin compression and under performance. He has worked with dozens of regional, national and international companies to redefine and add real value to the organization. Typically, year-over-year results turn into triple digit profit improvement. Lewis's approach is challenging and always brings about actionable change. In addition to his client work, he actively facilitates a number of CEO and Senior Leadership roundtables, as well as educational programs such as REDI.

Lewis is an inspiring teacher and mentor, empowering employees and leaders to innovate and exceed performance metrics. He has a history of providing companies and organizations with immediate and long-term success.

Lewis graduated with a degree in Political Science and History from Concordia University and completed the Stanford University Graduate School of Business in the Finance and Accounting for the Non-Financial Executive program.

www.rudyandassociates.com

Made in the USA
Monee, IL
17 May 2020